PURSUING JUSTICE:

One Woman's Life of Rebellion, Resistance and Resilience

Ruth A. Brandwein

Ruth Brandwein

ISBN: 978-1-962849-21-0

Dedication

Past—In loving memory of my parents, Charles and Kate Solin

Present—My children, Lorena Epstein and Garth Brandwein

Future—My grandchildren, Sara and Alex Epstein, Elise and Emma Brandwein and generations to come

Table Of Contents

Table Of Illustrations

PROLOGUE:

The Escape

I'M IN THE AIR! I'M FLYING! I'M FINALLY FREE. On a plane at 30,000 feet, looking down at the white, billowing, blanketing clouds. I see nothing below—no dirt, no crowds, just a blanket under a brilliant blue sky. I had made it! I was free! I had too escaped with my four-month-old son and three-year-old daughter. And I was on my way to Seattle. Why Seattle? He would never find me there. I had to disappear after he tried to kidnap Lorena.

Months before, when I was pregnant with Garth, Mel went to a New Year's Eve party, leaving me home to care for our daughter so he could meet a new girlfriend. Shortly after that, he told me he wanted to move out. In our six-year marriage, I had twice tried to leave, and he cajoled me back each time. The second time I thought I was losing my mind, I had resolved I could not try to leave him again, but if he ever left, I would do nothing to stop him. So, when he said he was leaving, to his surprise, I didn't beg him to stay. I had supported us since I graduated college, and he had decided to become "an artist." When he moved in with his girlfriend, he "graciously" allowed me to sell our loft and keep the proceeds. Of course, we did not own it, but in those days, you could get some cash if you found another tenant. They would pay you for the tip that the apartment would be available and whatever furnishings you had. We had some second-hand appliances, many plants, and a mattress on the floor. This cash was to support me until Garth was born and I could resume working. Where I would live was an open question.

Soon after Garth was born, Mel came to visit. "I got a used VW bus, and we're going to San Francisco to meet up with my old guru.

You and the kids are coming along." Somehow, once he had walked out of my space, it was as though a fog lifted from my head. I could think clearly instead of going along with everything he wanted like a "dutiful wife." "No, I'm not going," I told him. "O.K. I'll take Lorena, we'll have joint custody, and I'll bring her back in six months." "No, I don't want you to."

I knew that was crazy. First, I didn't even know where they were going; I would have no address or phone number to keep in touch with my child (this was in 1964, long before cell phones). Second, he was already having her call his girlfriend, Mommy. Even if he did return, which was a question, I could see the scenario: "Lorena thinks Hetha is her mommy. They have bonded! She loves her. Don't you want what is best for your child?" No, I would never agree to this ridiculous scheme!

He threatened to take me to court and declare me an unfit mother. He admitted to entering and searching the apartment he had rented for me while I was in the hospital and stealing my journal. I had just begun putting down thoughts and fantasies and feared how they could be misinterpreted!

Now it was summer. The lower East Side was rank with garbage, gangbangers in the street, simmering days and humid nights, and no air conditioning. Through my dad I learned about the Committee for Non-Violent Action (CNVA) peace farm in Connecticut, run as a commune. How great to get out in the country with the kids for a couple of weeks! I took a bus up there, but as a responsible parent, I sent my husband a postcard telling him we were away for just a couple of weeks and when I would return.

It was idyllic. Lorena and I had the job of milking the goat every morning. The grass was green, the air was clean and smelled of fresh hay instead of diesel fumes, and I could relax for the first time in years. Then, to my horror, my husband showed up with his girlfriend on their way to California. He wasn't interested in our son, who was still an infant, but he pushed me hard and physically yanked a screaming three-year-old out of my arms and got her into the car. I ran and tried to grab the keys out of the ignition but could only get the license number. Was I going to lose my daughter?

The peaceniks there stood aghast but did nothing to try to interfere. It wasn't their battle. I called the cops, and this is one of the only times I have been glad for the traditional family values of young children belonging to their mothers. After all, we had no divorce or even separation papers. Technically Mel had as much right to her as I did. When they stopped him, however, they found a concealed weapon (a blackjack) in his glove compartment. So, they detained him and called me. Arriving at the police station, I found my daughter peacefully sucking on a lollipop.

That's when I knew I had to get away, or he would seek revenge, take the children, and God knows what else he would do to me.

I found a lawyer through the peace movement who, I suspect, some years later was involved in hiding the Weather Underground fugitives. But he saved my life. He said, "Yes, you could lose your children. You guys have been smoking pot; you live in a barely furnished loft on the Lower East Side. But he wouldn't get them either. The Court would probably send them into foster care."

That was not going to happen! I was not going to lose my children. Then he advised, "If you're going to go underground, don't even think of going to New Jersey, Florida, or California. Within a week, you'll likely bump into someone who knows you, and he'll learn where you are."

So, I looked at a U.S. map. I knew I couldn't survive in the South and didn't want to get buried in the Midwest either. That left the West Coast. California was out, so it was either Oregon or Washington. Somehow, I knew there was a university in Seattle. I didn't know about Portland, so Seattle it was.

My parents were on vacation, so I borrowed $200 from Uncle Herb. I took the kids, one suitcase, whatever money I had left from the apartment sale, and the $200, and took a bus and stayed overnight with some new friends on Staten Island. From there, we took another bus and train to Newark Airport. I was afraid to go from either Kennedy or LaGuardia. I used a pseudonym. In those days, you didn't need an I.D. to board a plane. There was a sweet young guy at the CNVA farm whose last name was Moore, so I called myself Ruth Moore.

In those days, the stewardesses (that's what they were called) were not particularly friendly to a single mother with two babies. They were more interested in flirting with the businessmen smoking cigarettes in the back of the plane. We finally landed in Seattle, and I was still on my adrenalin high from having gotten away. I flagged a cab and said I wanted to go to Seattle to a low-priced hotel. I knew that it would be deadly to be stuck out in the suburbs without a car. Besides, I was a city kid. The driver took me to a place on First Avenue, which wasn't what it is like now. It was Skid Row, and the working girls stood out in front in the middle of the day. "No, I don't want to go here--take me someplace else." So, the cabby took me to another cheap hotel on Pike and 9th, way before the convention center was built. I didn't know it, but that was another street for prostitutes.

I was fearful but somehow elated that I had taken my life into my own hands and gotten away from the man I believed would have destroyed my sanity or my very life.

Before I had left NY, my lawyer had also advised me how to contact my folks. "Don't be surprised if he tries to jimmy open their mailbox to find your return address," he warned me. Instead, I would write to my parents and enclose the sealed envelope addressed to my folks, with no return address and enclose it in an envelope I would send to some friend of theirs in Florida, whom he did not know. They would then send my letter to my parents with their return address. A clever subterfuge I hoped would work. Now, I just had to figure out where to live, how to make a living, and how to protect myself and my babies. I'll tell you about that in Chapter 5, but first, let me explain how a nice smart Jewish girl from Brooklyn found herself in this situation.

PART I
MY ORIGINs

CHAPTER 1
From Shtetl To Brownsville

To know who I am, you need to know where I came from—who the people were who shaped my early life, in other words, my family.

I'll start with my mother Kate's parents. Her father, Grandpa Charlie, was born in a small village, a Jewish *shtetl* in Poland, in the latter part of the 19th century. (He was 64 when he died in 1952, so he would have been born in 1888). I might have heard the name of that village, but it wasn't vital for me to remember it at the time. When he was young, his family moved to Lodz in the Galicia part of Poland, which at that time was part of the Russian Empire. He was part of a significant internal migration of Jews, affected by the *Haskalah,* the Jewish Enlightenment of the 19th Century. Modernizing Jews moved from the *shtetls* to the cities, primarily Warsaw and Lodz. Lodz was a major textile center, and Grandpa soon was working in the mills. I think he met Grandma Gussie then. He left for America in 1904, and the family story is that he had to get out of town because he had been a member of the Socialist Bund. Russia experienced a failed revolution in 1904. The story is probably true because Grandpa was always siding with the USSR when I was a kid. Mom said he was never a card-carrying Communist—good thing because that was during the McCarthy period, but he and my dad, a Norman Thomas democratic Socialist, always got into arguments. Dad's Socialists hated the Soviets because of Lenin and Stalin's advocacy of violence. But Dad's politics is a later story.

My Maternal Grandparents: Charlie and Gussie Berkowitz

Grandpa Charlie came to America through Ellis Island, like millions of others, when immigration was encouraged because America was growing industrially and needed workers. He moved to Paterson, New Jersey, which, with its incredible waterfalls, was a major mill town. There, he and Gussie worked in the silk mills. Grandpa Charlie, whose Yiddish name was *Shaya* and was still called that by the older generation, was quite a character. I loved his skipping down the street with me as a kid, even when he was an "old man" at about 60. He had a crazy little toy terrier named Skippy who would jump on everyone. As I entered puberty, he was always sniffing my genitals and had this red thing sticking out (which, only years later, I realized was his erection!)

One of Mom's stories about him from when she was a kid was his booze-running during Prohibition. He'd make gin in the bathtub and transport it in the hollow under the back seat on which Mom and her kid brother Alexander (later changed to Berk) sat. When I was a kid, he had two means of livelihood. One was selling jewelry to friends from his vest pocket. He'd get orders of what someone needed—an engagement ring, a watch, or whatever, and go into Manhattan on the ferry to the jewelry exchanges down on Canal Street, buy a few selections on consignment, sell one and return the others. His other work was much more interesting. He ran a "joint," a probably illegal gambling establishment where other old Jewish guys would pay a fee (or maybe he got a rake-off from the winner) to sit and play pinochle or poker. They would be so wrapped up in the game that they wouldn't go home for dinner. Grandma Goldie (by then he was long divorced from my mother's mother Gussie), who was a great cook, would prepare and bring down some delicious smelling stuffed cabbage with raisins, homemade gefilte fish, or chicken soup with *kneidlach*, or other delicacies which they would pay for and keep playing while they ate.

When Grandpa Charlie died—of "clogged arteries," the funeral procession was one of the longest anyone had seen in Paterson. Everyone knew Shaya. After the funeral, several men, many Grandma Goldie didn't even know, would give her money—a return for a loan from Shaya.

My maternal grandmother, Gussie, or *Gitl* in Yiddish (my sister Gale is named after her), died tragically when only about fifty-two. Like Shaya, she had been a weaver. They both worked in the mills in Paterson, which at the turn of the last century was known for its silk mills. The famous Paterson silk mill strike occurred in 1913, and, of course, my grandparents were part of that strike of Jewish, Italian, and other young immigrants working twelve or fifteen hours a day for pennies. They were striking for an eight-hour day and better working conditions. Another family story is that Grandpa's older sister Tante Leah, also on strike, hit a policeman on the head with her umbrella. If you ever knew Tante Leah, with her big bosom and even bigger voice, you could believe it. Even in her eighties, she was one tough lady!

Grandma Gussie was a real radical, not just in her politics but in her personal life, just like Emma Goldman, whom she probably admired. She was among the first in her crowd to bob her lustrous auburn hair in the early Twenties when women wore it long. At one point, when my mother was about three or four and her brother about two, Gussie decided she could be an actress, so she and a married man she knew both left their spouses and took off for Hollywood.

Grandpa was left alone with the two kids. Mom told me they moved to Boston and lived with or next door to a friendly Italian couple. Mom remembered the delicious spaghetti sauce with lots of tomatoes and pork. Although Mom kept a kosher-style kitchen (no pork, shellfish, or meat with milk products) once a year, she would cook this pungent, garlicky dish. It was the only time of the year that our spaghetti sauce didn't come straight out of a can of Del Monte's.

Mom, at only four, had to be the little mother to her brother and companion to her distraught father. This didn't last long. Gussie, who did not make it as a movie star, returned, and Grandpa took her back. I think they were the family's black sheep, but the family felt sorry for Mom—little Katie—a sad, quiet little girl with cross eyes (from a bout with whooping cough as a young child.) One of Grandpa's three sisters (Leah, Esther, Sarah) had a house with a yard and collie dogs. Mom remembered happy memories of spending time with them; collies were always her favorite dogs. Years later, when I was little, she and Shaya were already divorced, and Grandma Gussie had a "boarder" living upstairs.

When I was about four years old, during World War II, I remember riding a bus up Madison Avenue in Manhattan with Mom and Grandma Gussie, to a doctor's office. The prominent specialists had offices in that area, so I thought it was called Medicine Avenue! Grandma Gussie was in continual pain, and the doctors couldn't figure out what it was. So, they decided it was in her head and put her in Bellevue, the "lunatic asylum." Mom was beside herself and unable to get her mother out, but Uncle Berk, her younger brother in the army, got a leave and released her with the help of the Red Cross. Soon afterward, she died—of uterine cancer, which they finally diagnosed at the autopsy. To the end of her life, Mom hated and distrusted psychiatrists.

This was a tough time for Mom. I remember her almost fainting in the grocery store. She was teary and hollering at Dad a lot. One year, when I was probably about four or five years old, we spent time with Mom's Tante Esther, Hannah's mother, who then had a big house in Rockaway Beach (Queens, NY) with a wraparound porch and big rocking chairs I'd climb into. In the summer, she would rent out upstairs bedrooms to beachgoers. Her husband, Uncle Arbe, a quiet little man, had wanted to move to the country, but Esther refused. "Where would my daughters find Jewish men to marry?" So, they compromised by buying this house with a large yard where Uncle Arbe had a vegetable garden. I still remember how delicious the tomatoes, cucumbers, and other fresh veggies tasted. Years later, Mom's cousin Hannah told me that at that time, Mom was having what was called a nervous breakdown. She told me we were there because Esther thought it would help Mom recover. I have no idea how long we stayed.

Mom's doctor advised her that the best antidote for her depression was to have another child. That's when my kid sister Gale was born. This was right after World War II, and housing was scarce. The four of us were still living in a three-room apartment up three flights of stairs in Brownsville, Brooklyn, where they had moved before I was born five years earlier. That sure helped Mom's mental state! I'll get back to that in the next chapter about growing up there, but first, I want to tell you about my father's family.

Dad's father, Henry, came to the United States from Bialystok, a large city in northeastern Poland/Russia near the Lithuanian border. The Jews from that area were known as *Litvaks*, contrasting with Mom's *Galitszeanas* family. Some great Rabbis had been Litvaks, so this group felt superior to those from Galicia. Their Yiddish pronunciation was also somewhat different. I used to say I came from a mixed marriage: Litvaks ate their potato *latkes* with sour cream, while those from Galicia preferred applesauce. I mixed them—tart and sweet, perfectly complementing the crispy, oniony potato pancakes.

My Paternal Grandparents: Henry and Anna Solinsky

Grandpa Henry emigrated in about 1904 or 05. He and Anna (*Chana* in Yiddish), a beautiful raven-haired young woman with big dark eyes and clear skin, moved to Brownsville after first settling on the Lower East Side in Manhattan, where many immigrants at that time landed after leaving Ellis Island. Before he died, I once interviewed him about those times. He said they first lived in a six-story tenement on the Lower East Side with no toilet. They had to go down to the courtyard to use the outhouse.

Grandpa Henry worked in the clothing industry in New York. He was a cutter—a more highly skilled and slightly better-paid job than those working the sewing machines (mostly young women). When I was little, Grandpa Henry used to make a matching coat and leggings outfit for my cousin Anita, who was about a year older, and me. He was a proud member of the ILGWU—the International Ladies Garment Workers Union- and an early member of the *Arbeiter Ring,* later known in English as the Workmen's Circle. This was not a union but a mutual benefit organization. These were common among different immigrant groups. They provided classes, loans (usually without interest—called a Free Loan Society), and burial benefits.

Henry, like Shaya, was a product of the Jewish enlightenment of 19th-century Europe. They freed themselves of the shackles of what had become a stultifying religion, turning to secular Judaism and a belief in human rights. Henry expressed it through unionism, and Shaya through communism. Anna's family, however, was religious. We have an old photo of my father, their first child, at age three riding a tricycle with long dark ringlets (*peyas*). On the sides of the image, under glass, are his actual curls cut off right after the photo was taken.

Anna tragically died of influenza in 1926 after giving birth to four children: my father, Jack, Harold, and baby Lily. Dad was fourteen; Lily was only four. Henry must have loved Anna very deeply. We have his love poems written to her in Yiddish after her death, translated into English by my father. So here he was, a widower in his late thirties, with four youngsters. On her deathbed, Anna made her sister-in-law, Tante Ida, promise to take care of her children. That Ida did, running between her house of three children and a husband who didn't or couldn't work, and Henry's family to cook, clean, and nurture both families. Dad always loved Tante Ida more than his stepmother. His mother's death made my father an atheist. He could not forgive God for letting her die, so he gave up on religion.

After a few years, Henry was introduced to Minnie, a widow his age with two children, whose husband also had died of influenza. This was not a love marriage but one of convenience. Grandpa Henry always favored his children, who he believed were more intelligent and more beautiful/handsome than Minnie's Belle and Al. Grandpa Henry was an attractive man; tall for his generation, straight-postured, and invariably well-dressed. Grandma Minnie was short and stooped with sparse grey hair, always looked dour and sour, wore laced-up black oxfords, and seemed old, although when I was a kid, she was probably only in her fifties.

How did Mom and Dad meet? Dad was unhappy at home with a new stepmother. At eighteen, he hitchhiked across the country, visiting the slaughterhouses in Chicago that eventually made him a vegetarian, and asking to spend a night in jail because he had no money for a bed for the night. After a year, he returned and visited his cousin Mary Smith, who lived in Paterson. Mary was a good friend of Mom's, and she invited them both to a party, where they met. Dad was nineteen, and Mom was eighteen. They spent the whole evening talking. Then Dad would send her love poems. He'd take the subway, ferry, and train out to Paterson to visit her. He was tall, dark, and handsome. Mom said he looked like an actor—maybe Robert Taylor. After three years, they took an apartment together, first on the Lower East Side, then in Queens near the World's Fairgrounds.

My Parents: Kate and Charles Solin

Mom never went to high school. Instead, after graduating eighth grade, she went to secretarial school for two years to become a bookkeeper, but I think she could have been a social worker. After the war was over, we finally were able to get our own telephone, and Mom used it! I still remember that black dial-up phone and our first phone number, Evergreen 5-6723. She was always the one to listen to her friends' sad stories. Her friend Belle had a husband who was a gambler and would give her only a small allowance, not enough to buy the food her growing and hungry boys needed. Sometimes Mom's friend Mary Smith would call from Paterson. I don't remember her sad story, but Mom would listen to her and commiserate. Dad's cousin Nettie had a husband who returned from World War II as a gambler. Mom would listen to her, and I would sit quietly listening. Mom used to say, "Little pitchers have big ears" and "Children should be seen and not heard." So as long as I was quiet, I could sit and listen. She said that's how I would learn things.

CHAPTER 2

Growing Up in a Three-Room Apartment

Brownsville is probably the only part of Brooklyn that hasn't been gentrified (yet.) It is south of Crown Heights, east of East Flatbush, and west of East New York. In the 1940s, it was a Jewish ghetto with four-story brick walkups and attached modest two-family houses with postage stamp front yards and concrete white painted planters standing like sentinels, some with faded sad-looking hydrangeas, on either side of the steps leading up to the front doors.

Ruth Age 2 in front of our first apartment in Brownsville

We lived at 41 Blake Avenue on the corner of Howard Avenue, in what my mother called the "nice" part of Brownsville. We were only four blocks from East Flatbush, a lower-middle-income neighborhood. Further east of us, the residents were poorer; the buildings were less cared for, with fewer two-family houses. Two blocks south of us was Livonia Avenue, darkened by the overhead subway line. (It was on Livonia Street in East New York, where the first Fortunoff store opened.) Six blocks east was Amboy Street, famous for the Amboy Dukes gang, and where my friend Goldie lived. Moving towards East New York, there were the beginnings of the "projects" where some African Americans (called Negroes) and Puerto Ricans started moving in. Around the corner from where I lived, on Grafton Street, stood P.S 156, a large older edifice where my father had attended elementary school and which I would as well.

Of course, there was no air conditioning, and the small apartments with little ventilation got unbearably hot. But we were lucky—we just climbed the one flight up to the roof. When I was very little, Mom and Dad would bring my crib mattress and put me to sleep up there while they sat and chatted. Dad put up a baby swing on some metal poles. As I grew older, he showed me the Milky Way, clear as there was less light pollution at that time. He even tried to plant some avocado pits that started growing into trees before the landlord found out and made him take them and the swing set down. Mom, always fearful, constantly warned me to stay away from the edge of the roof.

Ruth Age 3

The lobby of our building had a marble floor and four steps leading to the inner door. I was always trying to jump all four steps but finally managed to conquer three. On rainy days, the kids who lived in the building would congregate in the lobby, but on other days, after school and weekends, we girls would be in front of the house jumping rope, playing hit the penny, boxball, or using a pink Spalding ball to play "A my name is Anna, and my husband's name is Al, and we live in Alabama, and we sell apples" as we lifted a leg over while bouncing the ball. The challenge was to get through the alphabet without missing and being able to think of girl and boy names, names of places, and things for each letter of the alphabet. I never succeeded. Then there were jacks and pick-up-sticks. I don't know who introduced each of these. It was never me, but someone would, and we would all join in. The girls mostly played these games—although Stanley from the building diagonally across used to join us occasionally.

Then there was roller skating season. You put on the metal skates over your shoes and tighten the metal fasteners to the edge of your shoe with a skate key. At first, I would use just one skate, but I finally advanced to two and often had the scabs on my knees as proof of my many falls. After weekday school hours, Grafton Street was closed to auto traffic and became the kids' playground. The boys—and only the boys—would play softball, and we would all skate as the asphalt on the roadway was much smoother than the rough concrete sidewalks. Then out came the bikes and trikes. My mother finally let my dad buy me a (used) one-gear bike with the brakes on the pedals, but I was allowed to ride it only on that one street closed to traffic. I never did learn to be a confident bicyclist.

Our apartment, 7D, was on the top floor. In the other apartments lived Mrs. Levine, Mr. and Mrs. Lazarus, the Mednick family, with two beautiful daughters, Charlotte and Eleanor, five and ten years older than me, Mrs. Weinstein, and then the Millers moved in with Marilyn and Doreen, my friends and nemeses. Every evening at dinnertime Mrs. Lazarus, whose apartment was closest to the stairs and the dumbwaiter shaft, would open the door to the shaft and start knocking on doors to let us know the dumbwaiter had arrived. In the dumbwaiter shaft was a large garbage can, which the building superintendent would lift from the basement to every floor with a pulley.

Each of the mothers would bring out their garbage bags, depositing them into the large garbage can in the dumbwaiter, and when all were done, would close the door so it could descend to the next level. Of course, this was the time for the women to gossip and share the news. If anyone didn't answer their door, they would ascertain she was visiting her daughter or, for some other reason, was not home or sick. In this way, the community looked after one another. It was our village square.

Let me tell you about Marilyn and Doreen. They moved into an apartment on our floor when I was five or six. There were no playdates in those days, so you played with whoever was around. The only other girl in the building was Thelma Meshel, who lived on the ground floor and was older than me. Doreen was a year older but in the same grade. Two and a half years older, Marilyn was only one grade ahead of me. My first memory was meeting Doreen when she was sitting on the steps leading to the roof. She had a coloring book and was coloring in a picture, making the sky white and clouds blue. I told her she was wrong; it was the sky that was blue. That was our first fight.

I used to go to their house on Tuesday nights to watch the Milton Berle show because we had no TV. I had to come home right after that, but one night, a scary show they always watched announced, "This is a true story!" They persuaded me to stay and watch. It was about a little girl lured into an empty building by a big man and killed. I went home so frightened that after that, whenever I was walking alone in the street, I was afraid some big man was following me and would grab and kill me.

They got me into all kinds of trouble, and I, being younger and very naïve, went along with them. There were two incidents I am still ashamed of. Our family had gone to the circus, and I had asked for a whip, like the kind that they used to tame lions. Another girl around the corner named Madeline lived in one of the semi-detached two-family houses with steps leading up to a porch. I don't know how it happened, but we were walking past her house. I had my new whip, and Marilyn said, "Whip her with it," and I did! She cried, her mother called my mother, and I got in big trouble. "How could you be so stupid," my mother scolded.

Next door to our apartment house at the corner of Grafton Street lived an old lady with a little garden. A couple of years after that first incident, I was now eight or nine; we passed by and saw one big, beautiful sunflower. You need to know our neighborhood had few flowers or gardens. The Miller sisters said, "You're the littlest; you can climb over the fence and pick it." And I did! I think they probably took it home, and that was the last I saw of it, but I still feel guilty about that. Why was I always letting other people lead me? Why didn't I have the sense or strength of character to say no when I knew what was being asked of me was not right?

Then there was my stupid loyalty. In fifth grade, I was beginning to have some other friends, and they invited me to be in their "club." I said I would, but only if Doreen and Marilyn could be in it. They said no, so I didn't join. About a week later, I learned that another sixth-grade girl, also a club member, had asked Marilyn to join, which she and Doreen did, leaving me out! That was finally the end of that friendship.

Mom liked that our apartment was in the back of the building. She had not wanted an apartment facing the noisy street. She could look out the kitchen window and see one tree in the backyard of the two family house up the street. She said she needed to see some greenery. She hated living in Brownsville. She considered the people below her and uncultured. She had grown up in private houses, surrounded by grass and trees in Paterson. She also hated living in that tiny apartment with a small coat closet in the kitchen and another little clothes closet in the living room. When she was angry with my father, which was frequent in those days, she would berate him, complaining, "I should have married the butcher I worked for. I'd have a big house in Fairlawn now!" (Fairlawn was an affluent suburb of Paterson)

From the common hallway, you entered the kitchen, which was just big enough for a wooden table, later replaced with Formica, four chairs, a small Frigidaire with a tiny freezer just large enough for two trays of ice cubes and maybe one steak, a four-burner gas range on little legs and a sink. We always sniffed to ensure the pilot light wasn't out because escaping gas would be dangerous. The one window Mom liked to look out of opened to a clothesline where she would anchor wet clothes with clothespins. As a very young child I remember playing with those wooden clothespins because with their rounded tops and two legs I could pretend they were people. I also had a toy refrigerator with silver-colored wooden ice cubes that I set up on the side of our frig and pretended to be a mommy. Off the kitchen, to the left of the fridge, was a small bathroom with a toilet, sink, and tub. To the right of the refrigerator, a door opened to a small bedroom. My parents' beautiful blond wood bedroom set with a double bed including head and footrest, one-night table and matching lamp, dresser, and bureau (tall dresser) just about took up the room. From the window over the side of the bed, you could see the lights on Pitkin Avenue, two blocks to the north. Later they squeezed in a chifforobe—a standing metal closet to augment the minimal closet space in the apartment.

Another doorway led to the living room to the right of the kitchen table. It was the largest room, but it also had just one window, where mom had placed an ugly snake plant on the sill—the only plant hardy enough to survive in that setting. In front of the window was a big, easy chair with a standing lamp to its left. Because I was always younger, more awkward, and less socially adept, I would spend many afternoons curled up in that chair reading instead of going out and playing with the kids. Mom would always suggest books. First, it was *My Secret Garden* and *Little Woman.* When I got older, it was political novels by Upton Sinclair, Howard Fast, John Dos Passos, and Orwell. I first got my indoctrination to radical thought from those books. I always loved to read and had learned even before starting kindergarten.

On the other side of the living room was a studio couch where I slept. When Gale was born, a crib was added to that room. We did have a good folding bridge table and chairs, so on the rare occasions when family came over for dinner, they were set up in the middle of the living room. I don't remember them ever entertaining friends for dinner. Next to the couch stood the most valued piece of furniture, a full-size console radio with buttons to remember stations. Ours was turned on only to WQXR, the classical music station, and WNYC, the city-owned station with music and news. My favorite shows on Saturday mornings were "Let's Pretend" and "The Land of the Lost," sponsored by "Cream of Wheat is so good to eat, and we have it every day…" As I grew older, we could listen to Lucky Strikes' Hit Parade. At lunchtime, I always came home from school a half block away for lunch where mom was listening to the soap operas—Helen Trent, Wendy (something) Girl Reporter, and a couple of others, each fifteen minutes long.

One of the earliest memories I have of Mom was her ironing in the kitchen. She'd set up the ironing board in front of the front door, and in the summer, with no air conditioning, she'd leave the door open and iron in her shorts and a halter top. I also remember playing cowgirl. Uncle Harold, Dad's youngest brother, was stationed in Denver during World War II and sent me a cowgirl outfit! It had a bolero jacket with silver decorations and fringes. It also had a cowgirl skirt and boots, but maybe I imagined those.

As I got older, I remember returning from school in September, and there she'd be at the ironing board, listening to the radio. It was the pennant season, and we always rooted for the Dodgers. Maybe that's where I got my penchant for always siding with the underdog. The Dodgers always were snatching defeat from the jaws of victory, but everyone in our neighborhood went wild when they won. The Dodgers were like the Jews—underdogs, poorer than the Yankees, but with grit and determination. They were the first team to have a black player—Jackie Robinson, another underdog.

One year, I got the best present—an easel with a blackboard that opened to become a desk, with a scroll on the top with the alphabet. I would not play house, but school with my dolls and panda (not teddy) bear. I'd line them up sitting on the couch and teach them the alphabet. I guess I was fated to be a teacher.

In those years, our family all lived close by, as do many first generation families. Aunt Gertie, Uncle Al (Minnie's son), and their two kids lived just across the street and around the corner on Tapscott St. Grandpa Henry and Grandma Minnie lived a few blocks further in what we considered a really fancy building at 9720 Kings Highway. The start of Kings Highway was also the start of East Flatbush. Their building had a grand lobby and an elevator with a small, gilded gate that took you to their sixth-floor apartment. The only drawback of this large, two-bedroom apartment with a long hallway was that the back bedroom was only feet from the elevated train, which squealed as it rounded a bend at that point. My unmarried aunt Belle slept in that room. Dad's cousin Nettie also lived about two blocks away with her family.

Across the street and down Howard Avenue at 750 lived Grandma Minnie's sister Rose Weinstein, her husband, and their daughter Little Ruthie, so nicknamed because she was a full six months younger than me and *Bubba*, Minnie and Rose's elderly mother. They lived upstairs in a detached two-family home, and downstairs lived *Mima*, Bubba's sister, with her daughter Muriel. On many Saturdays and holidays when the weather permitted, all my father's family would gather in front of the house, the kids playing and the adults chattering. Sometimes Dad's brother Jack, who lived in Williamsburg, would also visit with his family. The first Passovers I remember were upstairs in that house at 750 Howard Avenue. A long table filled the dining room, and an extension was in the alcove behind it. As I recall, the women and girls sat at the end of the table in the alcove. I was furious because my cousin Joel, two years younger, got to sit with the men reading the *Haggadah* in Hebrew and ask the four questions. In later years, the Seder was held in Grandpa Henry's house, and I got to ask the four questions.

I turned six the year Gale was born, and my baby teeth started falling out, replaced by more prominent front teeth. I was losing my baby fat and becoming tall and thin. Gale was adorable and vivacious with curly red hair. She would be mischievous, but as the studious "big sister" praised for my high grades, I had to behave. That first summer after her birth, Grandpa Charlie arranged for us to vacation with them in Coney Island. He paid for it, as my parents had no money for vacations. We were given one large room in a *kuchalane*. This was a big rooming house with a large, shared kitchen in which each family had a specific section of the refrigerator.

Before going to Coney Island, we stopped in Paterson to pick up the grandparents. There I suddenly came down with measles. This was before the vaccine had been developed, and it was, and still is, a severe disease. My parents were apprehensive about their six month. old infant catching it, so the plan was to leave me there with Mom's cousin Rosie, who was a nurse. They would proceed to Coney Island, and I would join them when I recovered. I was a six year old left with Cousin Rosie, whom I barely knew. She was an uncommunicative fifty-year-old spinster and not known for her warmth, but she was a highly competent nurse. I was left in a big bed in a darkened bedroom. This was to prevent blindness, another danger of measles infection. I don't know how long I was there, probably several weeks. I didn't cry because I was a "big girl" and a "good girl" and was cautioned by my mother before they left not to cause any trouble. But I imagined they were all having fun while I was here all alone. Only years later, this memory came up in therapy, and I realized my subsequent fear of abandonment emanated from that traumatic experience.

Fortunately, I fully recovered and was taken to Coney Island, where I had a great summer—learning to swim, hanging out with many kids, going to Steeplechase, and walking the boardwalk every evening. Grandpa Charlie would put me on the brightly colored carousel, with a cheerful calliope and big horses that moved up and down. I always caught the golden ring, which gave me another free ride! Only later did I realize Grandpa probably paid the guy who ran it to remove several other rings so the golden ring would appear when it came to my turn!

I tasted my first soft custard, pizza, and Shatzkin's potato knishes that summer. Because Dad had a month's vacation, he was there a lot, and when he was working, he'd take the subway and get there at about 5:00. Mom would take baby Gale and go home to start dinner while Dad took a swim and watched me. That's the year he taught me how to swim. I loved the beach and swimming ever since.

After Gale outgrew the crib, Mom and Dad decided they wanted to have the living room to sit in during the evening. By now, they also had a record player attached to the console. I remember hearing Yma Sumac, the South American singer with a voice covering four octaves, Marais and Miranda, singing South African folk songs and some classical pieces like the Hungarian Dances, which I danced to around the living room. Some years later, they replaced the studio couch with a new invention popular at the time—a sofa bed—in which they slept while Gale and I shared the double bed in their bedroom.

I started dancing lessons, first ballet at the HES (Hebrew Educational Society, the settlement house at Hopkinson Avenue about eight blocks away) and later at the Walter Pritchard School of Dance up Howard Avenue toward Crown Heights. Mom loved modern dance. During the Depression she had taken lessons with Martha Graham through the WPA (Works Progress Administration, a New Deal program supporting artists.) I remember first dancing in The Nutcracker at the HES recital. The mothers all had to make our costumes, blue with short skirts. I continued with modern dance lessons for several years but was self-conscious because dancing gave me calf muscles, and I thought my legs looked fat. At the time, I was one of the tallest girls my age and envied the other petite dancers. I continued with modern dance through high school and my first year of college. That summer, I got a job as a dance counselor at a girls' camp. My ambition was to be a dancer and choreographer, but Mom talked me out. "That's a tough life."

In fourth grade, I was signed up for the afterschool Yiddish class at the *Sholom Aleichem Folkshul* in a basement on Tapscott Street. Dad was a Yiddishist—he was not religious but committed to Jewishness and the Yiddish language. We were to address our teacher as *chaver* (friend.) I learned to read and write Yiddish, but after two years I rebelled. That's when mom signed me up for piano lessons. We didn't have a piano, but there was a studio on the second floor of a Sutter Avenue storefront, where the lessons were $1 a week, and you could practice on their old (and battered and out of tune) pianos in their practice rooms. When I graduated elementary school, Grandpa Henry gave me a used upright piano, so now I could have a teacher come to our apartment, and I could practice on a halfway decent piano. It didn't help. I took lessons on and off for about four years but never showed much talent. Although Mom and Dad were always short on funds, they tried to provide me with opportunities to enrich my life.

As a teenager, Dad had hitchhiked twice across America to get out of the house where his new stepmother and step-siblings were ensconced. He visited the slaughterhouses in Chicago and was so revolted by the carcasses, blood, and dirt that he vowed to become a vegetarian. After several failed attempts, he became a vegetarian about the time I was born. Mom prepared meat for us but agreed to prepare separate food for him. Was it passive aggression? She would prepare the simplest fare—eggs or cottage cheese. She never made a vegetarian dish for the whole family. Dad never complained, insisting on one large carrot, scrubbed, not peeled, to retain the vitamins with each dinner.

In addition to his vegetarianism, Dad also studied Esperanto, a language created in the late 19th century to bring about peace in the world. The idea was that if we all spoke a common language, we'd all get along, and there would be no more wars. It was not universal, though, as the language roots were limited to European languages. Dad was also a Socialist, a follower of Norman Thomas, who ran unsuccessfully for President several times, following in the footsteps of Eugene V. Debs. Debs and Thomas were democratic socialists, believing in evolution rather than revolution to bring about a world of equality where the means of production and distribution would be democratically controlled rather than by wealthy individuals.

One of my early memories was standing on the corner of Blake Avenue and Grafton Street with Dad, handing out fliers for Norman Thomas for president. That would have been in 1948. Only several years later, I learned I had been handing out fliers for Thomas rather than Henry Wallace, who ran as a Progressive that year.

Dad worked for the City of New York. He finally had graduated from City College with a chemistry major after being expelled from Brooklyn College for participating in a rent strike and briefly studying engineering at Cooper Union. He started working for the Health Department but then switched to the License Department, where he pounded the streets daily, inspecting bars, pool rooms, and secondhand shops. He was probably the only inspector who was too honest to accept bribes, or even a cup of coffee, in return for a favorable report. He did accede to peer pressure and, like them, would quit at 4:00 p.m. rather than work until 5:00 because they said he was making the rest of them look bad. Worker solidarity, in this case, trumped his penchant for following the rules.

I remember once when we were getting new linoleum for the kitchen floor. When the linoleum installer asked Mom what Dad did for a living, and she responded, he made a crack about how much he was getting under the table. Furious, Mom said, "Yeah, that's why we're living in this three-room walkup!"

During the war, instead of being drafted, Dad used his chemistry background to get a temporary job with the federal government producing chemicals for the war effort in a factory on Staten Island. At this time, we did not own a car, so he had to take the subway, ferry, and bus to get to Staten Island. This meant leaving very early in the morning and getting home quite late. I was about four, and I loved my Daddy and missed him. So, one morning I moved a chair over to the door, climbed up on it, and put the chain on so he couldn't leave! Of course, he did, but gave me a big hug before leaving.

After the war, Dad became a pacifist (or the war made him realize he was) and joined the War Resisters League. Between that, working with others to try to start a cooperative in Brownsville, and his socialism, he went to lots of evening meetings. Then he decided to go back to Cooper Union at night for a degree in sculpture. Dad was a gifted artist, and this must have been satisfying to him, holding a dull job and having a difficult family life. For Mom, however, this added to her constant anger and nagging. She probably suffered from post partum depression and felt her life was disappointing. She had fallen in love with Dad when she was only eighteen; he was movie star handsome, had political values she admired, and wrote letters filled with poetry. They began living together three years later. Dad didn't believe in a conventional marriage, but they told everyone they were and always celebrated the date they began living together as their anniversary. Mom got pregnant and wanted to get married. Dad still refused, so she had an abortion. A few years later, when she became pregnant with me, he finally relented, and they were legally married in a civil ceremony. That's when they moved to Brownsville to be near Dad's family.

Now, with two kids, a tiny apartment, a small income, and a husband lacking ambition, she was angry at the man she had admired for his idealism. She still loved him, but her illusions had been shattered. Dad was not a "go-getter," not interested in making money or material things, and although he loved his children, he did not see his role as bettering the family's situation. He was a diligent worker, never missing work, and the job came with a pension and four weeks' vacation. He would contribute to various progressive causes, like the Spanish Civil War refugees.

Once, Mom found a stub of his contribution and yelled at him, "I don't have money to buy the girls new coats, and you're giving money away to your causes!" Those days she did a lot of nagging and hollering. Dad mostly stayed silent, sometimes reading or ignoring her, but occasionally he'd get mad and slam a door or a cupboard. I don't remember if he raised his voice, but I think that is how I became afraid of men's anger. The house was small; there was no room to go and shut the door to argue. I just stayed quiet, as I was expected to do, but I saw and heard everything. When I was very young, I would take his part in my mind, angry at her for being so mean to him. As I got older and understood Mom's situation, I sided with her.

Years later, a crisis occurred because of Dad's principles. That was the closest Mom ever even contemplated a divorce. Dad had worked for the New York City License Department for many years and would soon be eligible for a generous pension. As he was thinking about retirement, he decided it would be wise to move back to the Health Department, brushing up his skills so he could get a job in a hospital after retiring from city employment. This was now the late 1950s, and the country was still in the grip of the McCarthy era.

New city employees all were required to sign a loyalty oath. He was expected to sign because he was moving to a different department, but my dad stood on principle and refused. Not that he was "now nor ever had been a Communist," but he believed in civil liberties and didn't believe they had a right to ask for his loyalty. Mom went berserk! "You never made any money, but at least we knew you would have a pension! Now you're going to throw that away!" She was furious and frightened about their future. I sided with him, admiring him for sticking to his principles. Gale sided with Mom, looking at the practical side. Dad was a stubborn, principled idealist, but he was not stupid. He contacted his union and the ACLU. They both backed him; in the end, he kept the new job and did not have to sign!

I should tell you a little about the McCarthy era and how it affected our family. The House Un-American Activities Committee and McCarthy's Senate Committee were cross-examining anyone who had any leftist leanings or background. People who had been against the Fascists in the Spanish Civil War were under suspicion as were many who, during the Depression, had joined movements for equality, including the communist-front organizations. In this fever and fervor, many saw little difference between Communists and Socialists. I remember it wasn't a good idea to wear anything red for a while! Although Dad had never been a Communist, Mom was scared because of his involvement in so many progressive organizations. The Rosenberg trial ended with the first people convicted and executed for treason in peacetime—and they were Jewish! Mom cautioned me never to sign any petitions or repeat anything said in our home. That's when I learned to live in two worlds—the outside world and our family--so different from the mainstream.

After Dad finished the program at Cooper Union, Mom pushed him to work extra part-time jobs evenings and weekends. Then, when Gale started school, Mom got a job as a bookkeeper in the nearby conservative synagogue. Finally, we had enough money to move! We were coming up in the world, moving to a two-bedroom apartment in East Flatbush. Tante Ida and one of her daughter's family lived in the same building. Gale and I got to share a large bedroom with new twin beds. Mom let us pick out our matching bedspreads—a beautiful pink one with a beautiful design on the top and a pink ruffled skirt. By now, I was fifteen and starting my senior year in high school. I didn't want to change schools, so I took two subways to Thomas Jefferson High School in East New York every morning.

How did I get to be a high school senior at fifteen years old? When I started kindergarten, the school was still on the semester system, so I must have started in the spring. That year they changed it, so when I went into first grade, I did first and second grade in a year and a half. I was afraid of Mrs. Baum. She was mean. She would call on you with a question, and you had to stand up and call out the answer. I was a smart kid, but when she called on me for a simple arithmetic problem, I froze and started to cry. Of course, the mean boys, led by red-headed Melvin Steinhandler, called me "crybaby," an epithet that stuck with me for months. Throughout elementary school, I competed with Melvin to be the smartest kid in the class—I was never satisfied with being the smartest girl.

Third grade was better. Miss Shulman would start the morning by putting several arithmetic problems like $57+62=$ all over the front blackboard for us all to answer in our notebooks. Then she would often make me the "monitor" to make an A list and a D list of the kids who behaved or didn't while she went out in the hall and chatted with the other teachers for the next forty-five minutes. I was the "teacher's pet," but I didn't mind. Mom had advised me to listen to the teacher, be good and not worry about what other kids were doing or saying.

Mrs. Fox in fourth grade also liked me, and as I was always ahead of the class in reading, she would make me a monitor and send me around the school to the other classes for teachers to sign whatever forms were needed. I loved doing all that. In fifth grade, Miss Kameny was short, had dark hair, and was very kind. I got the part of Queen Isabella in the school play about Christopher Columbus, but the gown that Mom gave me to wear (an old one she had for years) was sleeveless. Miss Kameny didn't think that was appropriate, so she lent me her purple bolero jacket to wear over it.

My very favorite teacher was Mrs. Esakov in sixth grade. A terrible incident happened one Friday. On Friday afternoons, the boys and girls were separated, and all the boys from her and Mrs. Turk's class stayed with Mrs. Esakov to do woodworking or something while the girls from both classes went to Mrs. Turk's room for sewing. We were to be sewing aprons, apron envelopes, and chef hats, by hand, with our names embroidered. Some of the girls had mothers who were seamstresses and did very well. I did not. My hands would be dirty, my stitches too big and uneven. I'm still not handy with such tasks.

We were allowed to chat quietly with our seatmates, and if we had a question, we were allowed to go up to the front of the room and ask the teacher our questions.

As I got up from my seat, the room was getting louder. Mrs. Turk saw me out of my seat and thought I was a troublemaker—me, the good girl and teacher's pet! She didn't know me and refused to listen to my explanation. She ordered me out of her class and told me to return to my room! How could I do that? All the boys were there. I'd be so ashamed. I wandered the halls for a few minutes, crying.

Finally, just before 3:00, when school would be let out, I abjectly returned to my classroom and, whimpering, told Mrs. Esakov what had happened. She was most sympathetic and must have had a good talk with Mrs. Turk because after that, whenever I had to go to her room for anything, she was super friendly to me. Of course, she never did apologize. At the end of the year, Mrs. Esakov gave me a book I treasured, and it still sits on my bookshelf. It was Robert Louis Stevenson's *Kidnapped* in hardcover in a slip jacket.

That year we were all given Sanford-Binet Intelligence tests in preparation for placement in junior high school classes. My parents were called to the school and told that my IQ was 159! I'm not sure if being told my IQ was a blessing or a curse. I've always believed that because I thought I was more intelligent than most people, I should be able to do just about anything I set my mind to. I also learned not to appear superior—that doesn't win friends. Knowing my IQ was also a negative. After all, I always felt compunction to accomplish because I should be able to. I thought I would be remiss not to fulfill my potential.

The school suggested to my parents that I enroll in Hunter High School in Manhattan instead of going to the local junior high school. Hunter was a special school for advanced children, but my mother didn't want me traveling an hour each way to school by subway. I had already been taking the subway by myself to the allergy doctor, and the following year my friends and I would often travel into the city by ourselves. But Somers Junior High School 252 was a newer East Flatbush school with a strong reputation and a progressive curriculum. My parents (really my mother—I don't think Dad was very involved in any of this) decided that was where I would go, and I was enrolled in the Special Progress class. That program was for children who tested highly to do the three years of junior high school in two. So between having skipped a half year in second grade, a year in junior high, and having a birthday at the end of April, just before the cutoff for the year, I entered tenth grade in high school when I was thirteen. I was usually the youngest in my class.

Junior High was fun, although on the first day of school I noticed all the girls were wearing lipstick. Mom refused to let me wear it, but the following year, when I entered ninth grade, she changed her mind and said I should. I obeyed her both times. I had two sets of friends: Goldie Kramer, who I am still friends with, lived on Amboy Street, the famous street of the former "Amboy Dukes." She lived with her parents and sister in a dark, first-floor apartment in the "bad" part of Brownsville. My other friends, Sheila Steinberg, and Sondra Zipkin, lived in East Flatbush, near the school. My wardrobe had changed, and I started wearing a bra, tight skirts, neckerchiefs, and sweater blouses like the other girls. In ninth grade, our homeroom teacher called a few of us aside and chastened us for wearing bras with very pointy cups. That was the style, and some of the girls shrugged off her criticism, but I took it to heart and wore more modest bras and less revealing sweaters.

At the end of ninth grade came the prom. I liked Martin Itzkowitz, who was smart and a good fiction writer. I hoped he would invite me, but days passed. Mom wanted to be sure I could go, so she spoke to a friend who knew Milton Green's mother. Milton, who was in my class, invited me. I didn't want to go with him because I didn't like him and thought he looked nerdy, but Martin hadn't asked me, and I wanted to go, so after a day's hesitation, I accepted. Martin went with Letitia Heller. My crush on Martin continued in high school when we were both on the staff of the Jeffersonian, a literary magazine. Many years later, I met him at a party at a friend's home in Manhattan, where he admitted he had also had a big crush on me all those years ago.

Then came high school. Our street in Brownsville was on the dividing line between Thomas Jefferson in East New York and Samuel J. Tilden in Flatbush. Depending on the demographics each year, sometimes our side of the street went to one, sometimes the other. In 1953 the kids on our side of the street were slated to attend Jeff. My mother wanted me to attend Tilden, which had a middle-class, primarily Jewish population. Jefferson was in a poor neighborhood with a mixed population of Jewish, Italian, and Black kids.

Mom had a plan. Through someone she knew who worked for the schools, she learned that if I wanted to enroll in a class that was not offered in Jefferson but was in Tilden, I could attend there. So, unbeknown to me, she enrolled me in a violin class. Guess what? Jefferson had started one for the first time, so there I was on the first day of classes at Jeff in a violin class. I didn't know how to play, didn't even know how to tune the damn thing, which took me most of the hour. I finally dropped it after the first semester, but I will never forget that violin passage from Beethoven's Seventh I sawed through.

The school had tracks—honor school and honors classes, in which I was enrolled, where many of the Jewish kids were. Then the commercial track where the Italian and Jewish girls slated to be secretaries were enrolled. Finally was the general track, with vocational courses, no Regents classes that prepared one for college, and less committed teachers. Miss Meehan, our sophomore history teacher, had us reading Plato's *Republic*, and in English that year, we read *Hamlet* and a trilogy of war stories, *The Red Badge of Courage*, *All Quiet on the Western Front*, and *The Trojan Women*. Toward the end of the spring semester, I was chosen to participate in a voluntary late Friday afternoon group with Dr. Cohen, which was not a formal class. The twelve or fourteen of us sat around the room, and he had us read Greek tragedies, taught us the (then new) Heisenberg theory, and had us study current history and politics, preparing us for the college entrance exams. It was an extraordinary opportunity, and for two years, we were exposed to literature and ideas at an advanced university level.

I was growing and progressing intellectually beyond my years, but I was socially immature, one or two years younger than my classmates. Several girls had boyfriends, some of whom were in the army. I felt like I would never have a boyfriend. I believed no boys liked me and had no confidence in how to act around them. Then I met Mel Brandwein.

CHAPTER 3

Mel—Svengali or Sociopath? How We Met and Married

It was finally the end of my sophomore year of high school. I'm fourteen, 5'5" tall and have worn a bra for over two years. Mom is working, so I have to take Gale to the Hebrew Educational Society (HES), the settlement house on Pitkin Avenue, to register for the same three-week camp I attended for two years. I'm in line when a cute boy actually approaches me. He's not tall, but wiry with light brown hair, deep-set blue eyes, a pointed chin, and a winning smile. He's registering his kid brother Paul for the same camp. He goes to my high school but is not in the honors program. He's wearing a white tee shirt with the sleeves rolled up and in it he has a pack of Lucky Strikes. I tell him I'm going to camp in a few weeks. He tells me his uncles have arranged for him to go to Israel. I think that this would be fun and a little thrilling to have an experience with this boy who is so unlike me and who will soon be gone from my life.

So that's how it started. Mel was sixteen, and he was supposed to go to Israel because he and some other kids had gotten into trouble stealing something, and his uncles, both social workers, were able to arrange for him to make a new start in Israel. I wrote to him daily from camp, some days on my lilac and others on my light green stationery, with matching inks. Of course, he never did go to Israel, and we started dating when I returned.

Ruth at Summer Camp, Age 14

My parents insisted on meeting him. Although he could put on the charm, Dad disliked him from the first, but after he had left, Mom said, "With a boy like him, you'll never be poor. He's a real hustler." (Was that a jab at Dad?) She would prove right about the second but wrong about the first. For that first date, Mom said, "I want you to take her someplace where there are lots of people and lights." How clever was he? He took me for a walk to Eastern Parkway, where we sat on a bench as people walked by, cars with their headlights drove by, and we looked at the moon scuttling behind clouds. One night, he said something I thought was so romantic. "You're like a perfect clear glass flower with no color, and I will paint the color in you."

It was so exciting to meet his family. They owned a two-story house in East New York. They were so different from my uptight, square bourgeois middle-class parents! Mel was the oldest of five; next came Stan (Wolfie), then Ruthie, Alan, and Paul. Paul was the baby at about eight or nine years old and a little pudgy. He revered Mel, who was his protector. Stan was much taller than Mel's 5'8'; slender, with dark brown curly hair to Mel's straight light brown hair. Ruthie was tall, broad-shouldered, and awkward, with close-set eyes.

Alan was different from the others. Thin and quiet, he was the artist and had his bedroom off the kitchen. As I remember, Paul, Ruthie, and Stan shared one large bedroom, and their parents had the front room. Mel had his room upstairs with a door off the hall. The other door led to an apartment rented by the Perez family. Mel's mother, Jeanne, was a sweet woman who always appeared frightened, laughed inappropriately, and seemed not quite with it. By contrast, his father, Ben, was massive, a tall, heavy-set man who seemed to dominate the family with his voice and manner. I suspected he was violent, but I never actually witnessed it. He was an Orthodox Jew, and for the first time in my life, I observed someone put on phylacteries (leather bindings around one arm and a little box placed on the head) before his morning prayers.

Mel would take me to his room, where he would play classical music because he knew I liked it and pretended he did. How often did I hear Dvorak's *New World Symphony* and Tchaikovsky's *Pathetique*? We'd make out, kissing, and once, he touched my breasts when he got me on his lap. As a "good girl," my first reaction was to pull away and say "no," but he cajoled me. "Why not? Doesn't it feel good?" Yes, it did, so I let him fondle my breasts.

Now, in my junior year, I started living in two worlds. During the week, I was this honor student on the school magazine staff, getting

"A"s in all my classes (except chemistry), with a group of friends from Arista--the honor society, but on the weekends, I'd take the subway to Mel's house, and we'd hang out in his bedroom and make out. He was my secret, but at least I knew I had a boyfriend! I think it was that year that I started developing some self-mutilating habits. I would pull my hair apart at their split ends and start pulling them out of my head. He wanted me to pop the pimples on his back and, in return, would pop mine. I know that sounds disgusting, but we liked doing it. He also wanted me to shave my legs, so I did. When I got ingrown hairs, I'd pick on them.

I was only fifteen that summer, so I couldn't get a junior counselor job in the day camp up in the Catskills with my friend Sheila. The camp owner needed a mother's helper for his pregnant wife, who needed help with their two-year-old son. I had to get a work permit and was thrilled to have my first real job! I would live with the family and have two days off every four weeks. I think my pay was about $200 for the summer. I spent my first day off with Sheila. We had a great time going to Monticello, where I had mint chocolate chip ice cream for the first time. We went to summer stock that evening and stayed up all night talking. On my second day off, Mel came up, and we spent the day and night in his motel room when we started more heavy petting.

Senior year was great! I had a story published in the Jeffersonian, and I did the choreography and danced in "Bali Hi" for the production of *South Pacific*, which we performed in the school auditorium. I wasn't yet sixteen, but many of my friends were older, and this was the year of Sweet Sixteen parties. I had lot of fun and danced with many boys. Jacob Lipkind, tall, handsome, and the smartest boy in our class, even took me home once.

I was volunteering in the school library and still getting straight A-grades while starting to think about college. For the first time, the Ford Foundation was giving out scholarships. I always tested well, especially on the NYS Regents exams, where I usually scored in the high nineties. I took the scholarship exam and dreamed of going to UCLA, which I read about in a magazine. In the back of my mind, it would be a way to extricate myself from the relationship with Mel, but I'd never admit that to my parents, who were unhappy with our relationship by now. I was getting home later and later on Saturday nights. That year Mel turned eighteen and bought a big used Buick. We'd make out in the front seat. I was still a virgin, but we had now advanced to everything short of intercourse.

One night, when I got home at 3:00 a.m. Mom was furious and said, "Talk to your father." Dad was never very involved, and I think if he had put his foot down, I would have respected that. I wanted him to protect me. However, when we started talking, I manipulated him into a political discussion, and he never even tried to discipline me. I felt very smug about how I had wiggled out of that, but deep down, I was disappointed in him.

Mel and I had one big fight. After he saw me with my stage makeup in *South Pacific,* he wanted me to wear a lot of eye makeup and rouge. I put it all on but didn't like it, so I got mad and scrubbed it off. Then he got angry and stormed out of my house. I was relieved and thought maybe now I could end the relationship. Then Mom said, "Oh, it's just a lover's quarrel; you'll make up." I felt trapped.

Mom didn't want me to go out of town to college. She was afraid Mel would follow me, and she wouldn't have any control over me. She didn't know she had already lost control. Then, the word came down that the faculty had made some errors in giving the Ford Scholarship exam, so the results were nullified. My parents had no money to send me away to school; besides, my dad had gone to the city colleges, which were fine educational institutions. And I was only sixteen. I would live at home and attend Brooklyn College, only a few subway stations away. I don't remember any school counselors even suggesting Cornell or Barnard; neither I nor my parents knew enough to inquire. I received many honors and the Mayor's medal when I graduated high school. I came in 37th in the state on the Regents Exams and probably could have received a scholarship to a prestigious school.

High School Graduation at Age 16

The summer I graduated, my parents, who had finally bought their first car two years before, wanted to take a month's trip to Florida. I had no interest in spending all that time with my parents and kid sister, but they were not about to leave me alone in Brooklyn with Mel. It was the first time I had been to the South, and my father, who was involved in civil rights, pointed out the segregated bathrooms and water fountains along the way. In Miami Beach, we stayed in a motel, and one evening I flirted with the waiter at a restaurant. The next day I saw him on the beach. We went in for a swim. He said he was from Tennessee. When I told him I was Jewish, he looked at me perplexed and innocently inquired, "But where are your horns?" Growing up in a Jewish environment, I was shocked that others had such misconceptions about Jews.

On the way back, we took a different route, and at twilight, we were approaching the Okefenokee Swamp. My parents were worried about traveling through there at night and looked frantically for a motel. Finally, we found Chief Tomacheechee Motel, an old-style one with separate little cabins. It seemed an odd place. We had one large room with two double beds and a rocking chair. My mother screamed when she saw a giant cockroach on the wall over the bed—a palmetto bug. Dad killed it, but Mom made him move the bed away from the wall so none would fall on us in our sleep.

The following morning as we loaded up the car, we looked around and saw that all the other families leaving were Black. My parents realized the owner had been very kind and taken a real chance to let us, a white family, into his motel. These experiences marked the dawn of my understanding of prejudice, segregation, and injustice to people of color.

When the trip ended, the first thing I wanted to do was spend time with Mel. My parents feared what might have happened if I had stayed in Brooklyn, but little did they know what happened when we returned. Mel had kept telling me about another girlfriend he had in Hempstead named Mona, who was "putting out" for him. Instead of getting angry because he was seeing another girl, I was determined to keep him, and I guess I wanted to get back at my parents for making me take the trip, so that night, in his bed, in his room, I lost my virginity. Looking back, I have no idea if she really did that or if there even was a Mona.

I started Brooklyn College at sixteen as an elementary education major. The year was 1956. I had no idea what I wanted to do with my life. All the Jewish girls who didn't get married after high school and became secretaries until their first kid was born went to college and majored in education. As my mother advised, it was a good job to fall back on if anything ever happened to your husband and you had to go to work.

That summer, I lied about my age. I had just turned seventeen and got a private girls' camp job. You had to be eighteen, but I was already entering my sophomore year in college, so they never questioned my age. I chose between that and Camp WelMet, a settlement-house camp that hired many group workers as counselors, many of whom later would become social work professors at Columbia University. How different might my life have been had I gone there? But Mom advised working at the private camp. She said, "You'll probably be working with poor kids when you teach, so here's a chance to be around rich people."

All the counselors were specialists and also oversaw a "bunk" of just four girls. I was the dance counselor and had adorable seven and eight-year-olds. I created some innovative dance activities with girls of different ages. Then, at the camp show, we put on an original musical. The drama counselor wrote it, the music counselor provided the songs, and I did the choreography. I was having a great time, but Mel came up on one of my days off. We spent the day in his motel room. Once again, I was torn between a life of fun, creativity, and meaning and what I thought I needed to do to have a man.

By my second year of college, having completed required courses, including an innovative integrated social science yearlong course where we read primary source materials in sociology, psychology, anthropology, and political science, I was taking education courses that I thought were vapid.Actually, Helen Hafner's course in child development was terrific, and I did an independent study with Edgar Z Friedenberg, a great scholar who guided me in visiting both general education and specialty high schools. Still, one class that taught us about opening windows and making the school environment pleasant made me decide to change majors.

I wanted to understand the meaning of life! So, I chose a combined major in philosophy, world literature, and Eastern religions. The only problem was that the college did not recognize combined majors. My counselor helped me by suggesting philosophy as my major, which required only eighteen credits (six courses) so I could take classes in the other two areas. I spent my last two years of college taking courses in Existential Philosophy, Zen Buddhism, Russian and Italian 19th-century novels, and an innovative seminar on Justice with faculty from English, history, and philosophy departments. I became an

Existentialist. I read Camus, Kierkegaard, and Sartre, wore my hair long, with white lipstick, a black beret, and a tan trench coat. I loved my Existentialism class with Prof Gerhardt and my Philosophy of History course with Prof Sprague. I could never figure out Phenomenology with Prof Cerf and crossed swords with Prof. Hospers in Ethics. He gave me only a B+ for my final paper. I'm convinced it was because I disagreed with him. Many years later, I learned he had been a vice-presidential candidate for the Libertarian Party!

Mel persuaded me to marry him when I was eighteen. His father, who delivered seltzer and beer on Long Island, had bought Mel his own route. So now, he argued, we could afford to get married. I didn't want to, but I loved him, so what could I do? My parents opposed it but feared losing me if they tried to stop me. Early in our relationship Mel had cautioned me that anything we said between us I was never to repeat to anyone. I was no longer confiding in my friends. Mel had isolated me from them and turned me against my parents. I participated in putting them down, perhaps as a way of surreptitiously standing up to my mother. I didn't feel I had anyone to confide in. I felt isolated and trapped but had no strength or self-confidence to say or do anything about it.

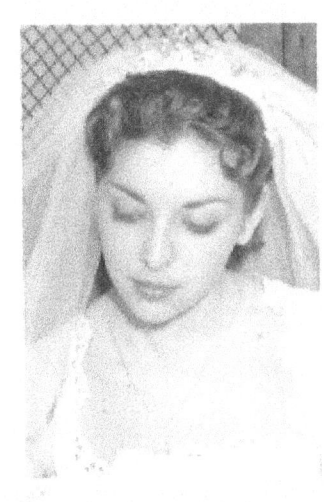

Signing wedding Katuba

So, we got married. The wedding brings even more painful memories. I secretly believed I could always get divorced. I didn't want my parents to spend a lot of money, so at the reception, I insisted on having just cold cuts, instead of a fancy dinner in the synagogue's party room. Sitting at the head table next to me during the dinner, Mel was already counting the checks people had given us. Afterward, he took some of the younger boys for a joy ride in his car. They were away for about an hour, to my shame.

We went to Lake Winnipesaukee in New Hampshire for our one-week honeymoon. I remember that Mel disappeared one day, and I had nothing to do but look through the local telephone directory. We rented a basement apartment in Flatlands, south of East Flatbush, and I spent the summer painting the walls and fixing the apartment up.

That fall, I was happily taking classes, and Mel was working. However, he succeeded in destroying the business within a year. This is how it happened: He thought he was smart and was always working the angles. He didn't want to be bothered delivering only half-crates of just six bottles of seltzer, so he gave up those customers, thinking he'd do better concentrating on those who ordered a whole case every week. The problem was that other deliverymen poached his territory by serving his former customers who wanted just a half-case. It wasn't long before he didn't have enough customers for the business to survive.

After a year, we moved to another basement apartment in a home owned by Hungarian immigrants. Mel's parents were now divorced, and he learned that their house mortgage had just been paid off. His idea was to have his mother bankroll him in a business. So, he and Jeanne flew to South Florida and stayed at my mother's cousin's motel in Hialeah (for which he never paid). He had left Jefferson in his senior year and went to a trade high school for cooking. I'm not even sure if he ever graduated, but he decided to buy a restaurant!

It was my spring break a week later, so he persuaded me to come down. I took my first plane ride on an Eastern Airlines propjet to Miami. While they were looking at businesses to purchase, I was reading *The Brothers Karamazov* and swimming 100 laps in the little motel pool. At the end of spring break, Mel persuaded me to stay instead of returning to school. I think I stayed another two weeks until they decided there were no businesses to buy, and we all went home.

When I returned, I planned to drop out for the rest of the semester, as I had already missed two weeks of class. The college counselor, who I think was my angel, persuaded me to stay. I wonder if I would have ever finished if I had dropped out that semester. I was taking an overload of six courses. He advised me to drop the two with the most readings and keep the rest. I did, and that semester got only a B average.

Before graduation, Mel undermined me in other ways. As he couldn't find a business to buy, he got his mother to stake him in starting an insurance brokerage. The first thing he did with his mother's money was to buy some nice new suits, a new Pontiac convertible, and clothes for me. He said we had to look successful. He was advised to join a bowling group to make contacts. He spent most of his time in the bowling alley. As a good wife, I had to help him succeed in business, so he had me make calls for him. The only insurance policy he sold was one to a cousin of my mother's. As graduation neared, he started going to the racetracks to make money gambling. I was obliged to go with him instead of working on my final papers. Despite his efforts to undermine me, I did manage to graduate Phi Beta Kappa as well as *magna cum laude*.

Fortunately, over the four years we were having intercourse I never got pregnant. At first, I was so young that I probably wasn't fully developed, as my periods were irregular. We were using the "rhythm" method, and it was just dumb luck that I could finish college before my children were born. Having that college degree would make all the difference in my future.

CHAPTER 4

Beatniks and Descent into Hell

When I graduated in 1960, Mel declared that now that, as a college graduate, I could earn more than he, and his having supported me for the last two years, it was my turn to support him so he could become an artist. Not wanting to be a "square" and fall back on gender roles and certainly not wanting to be a nag like my mother, urging my husband to make money, and wanting to be a good, compliant, "oriental type" wife, of course, I acceded. I was very much a product of the 1950s, having been told that although marriage was supposed to be a fifty/fifty proposition, it was actually the wife's responsibility to make it work.

My friend Myrna had always wanted to be a librarian. Brooklyn Public Library was recruiting librarian trainees. If you worked for the Brooklyn Public Library for a year as a trainee, they would pay for your librarian degree. Myrna was meeting the campus recruiter—did I want to come? I had gone to college because it was my parents' expectation, and I always excelled in learning. I had spent the last two years taking courses that had meaning for me—education for its own sake. Having no idea what I would do upon graduation, I went. As I liked little kids, I decided to be a children's librarian. I was hired and spent three months at the system's main library at Grand Army Plaza. My supervisor was Carol Kay, a brilliant, dynamic woman probably in her late 20s but already in a top position and a great role model.

I loved working with and for her and was given my own Children's Room at the Glenwood branch library on Flatbush Avenue after three months.

By now, we had moved again. Mel and I had started spending evenings and weekends in Greenwich Village, usually at Cino's coffee house on Cornelia Street, a hangout for gays, lesbians, and musicians. So, we (he) decided to move to the Village. We rented a large three room apartment at 10 Sheridan Square on the 14th floor, around the corner from Cornelia Street.

Now I had to commute every day an hour back to Brooklyn, but I loved living in the Village. We made lots of friends at Cino's. One was Ludwig Datane, a very young painter who had fled the home of his Nazi parents in Ridgewood, a German neighborhood in Brooklyn. There was also a Spanish family of two brothers and a sister who played flamenco guitar; a short, older Japanese-American woman named Taka Nokano, who lived with her teenage son in a 6th-floor walkup on McDougal Street and whose family had lost everything when they were interned during World War II; and a Greek man who did etchings and carvings that he said were what the ancient Greeks had done. He also had a very young boyfriend. In addition to Joe Cino, the owner, there was another Joe with a long scruffy beard and grubby clothes who acted like a "flaming" gay. He had lost a wife and son in an auto accident. Many nights some of these habitués would put on little shows while we drank grenadine and soda or *café au lait*.

This was my first introduction to the gay culture of the early '60s. We would also walk the streets ignoring the grime, auto emissions, and trash along the gutters, loving the excitement of the new discoveries, whether the Strand bookstore near Cooper Union, Washington Square Park, or a little jazz club on East 10th Street. The diversity of lower Manhattan was a revelation as we experienced different cultures within this mini-universe. Second Avenue still had Jewish delis and dairy restaurants; First Avenue was Italian; Avenue A had Ukrainian and Polish shops; Avenue B was primarily Puerto Rican, and Avenue C was mainly African American.

I also loved my job. I read to preschoolers at a weekly story hour; I got to review and order new books and remove soiled and torn books from the shelves. I discovered books for children about sex hidden behind the previous librarian's counter and shelved them among other books, so kids could take them out if they wished. My little act of rebellion! Because the library hours were nine-to-five, I had little to do until 3:00, when hordes of school children would suddenly descend, demanding books their teachers had assigned.

One morning I noticed the head librarian, a former nun whom I could never warm up to, was in whispered discussion with an elderly gentleman. Every so often, their gaze would turn to me. She took me aside when he left and asked, "Did you see the man I was speaking to? He's the priest from the Catholic school across the street. He thought your skirt was too tight." I think I replied something like he should mind his own business. Maybe it was tight because I had become pregnant.

Some mornings my nausea made me miss my subway, and I would arrive fifteen or twenty minutes late. I was reprimanded for being tardy and told I would never succeed if I didn't learn promptness. I didn't think it mattered, as the kids didn't come in until the afternoon, and I was the only one ever busy at the library. In my future career, I always had positions where I had flexible hours, often coming in at 9:30 or 10 a.m. and leaving at 7 or 8 p.m. It was a long walk from the subway station, and in January, I started wearing black tights under my skirt. We never wore slacks at work in those days. The librarian chastised me for wearing tights, so I would change to sheer pantyhose when I got to the library, on her time. Soon after, my pregnancy began to show, and I was terminated. In those days, you couldn't work as a teacher or a librarian when you were pregnant. I guess kids shouldn't know you could be capable of making a baby.

So now Mel had to work. He got a job delivering milk, but that didn't last long. He was always looking for angles and ways to make money the easy way. I'm not sure, but I think he removed names from his order book and pocketed what people had paid. At the library, I came across a book entitled *The Holy Barbarians* about the Beatnik culture of San Francisco in the 1950s. Mel read it avidly and decided we should eliminate our material possessions, get out of the capitalist consumer culture, and become beatniks. That was his rationale for not working and starting to sell our possessions so we'd have money to live on without him having to work.

When working at the library, I found two books about the Lamaze method. One was called *Childbirth Without Pain,* and the other was *Thank you, Dr. Lamaze.* I found a Lamaze trainer in the Village, and Mel and I attended classes that taught us the different steps of labor and how to breathe and relax one's muscles. I was determined to have my baby the natural way, without the use of any medications. I wanted to be awake and fully there when my child was being born. I also did not want an episiotomy. My obstetrician said he would wait to see if I could deliver without being cut, but if he saw the baby pushing against the opening at risk of brain damage, he'd immediately perform the episiotomy. I practiced diligently, relaxing my sphincter muscles.

When I delivered, the doctor said, "You melted like butter." I was the only woman on the floor who didn't have stitches and could walk and use the toilet right after delivery. I was also the only woman on the floor who was nursing. This was not yet a common practice in 1961. It was one of the most extraordinary life experiences to be up and conscious while delivering my child, hearing her first cry, and holding her. Mel wanted to name her Aurora Della Lisa but gave in to Lorena Lisa. The deal was that I could name the girl, and he would name the boy. Lorena was born on June 7, 1961. She was a beautiful 7 lb. 20" child with perfect red lips, ten tiny fingers and toes, smooth, sweet smelling skin, and deep blue eyes that turned dark brown. I was totally in love with her. One of my sweetest memories was nursing her while reading a philosophy book. Our obstetrician was a private doctor at Beth El Hospital. When we had asked about payment at our first visit, the doctor joked, "If you don't pay, we take the baby back."

Mel never did make the final payment, but I kept my baby. While I was in the hospital, I guess the rent hadn't been paid, so we had to move again. This time, Mel had found an apartment on the top floor of a private home in Park Slope back in Brooklyn. By now, we had sold my engagement ring, our wedding silverplate flatware, and some of the furniture we had bought for the previous apartment. The beautiful couch and chairs were never fully paid for. Mel had expected to sell a large insurance policy and get a hefty commission. I urged him not to buy until it came through, but as a good submissive wife, I went along with him. That furniture store eventually went out of business. Each time we moved, we left no forwarding address and either didn't have a phone or changed the number.

When Lorena was three months old, it was time for me to return to work. I never questioned that decision or thought I had any right to be able to stay home with my baby. I loved breastfeeding, but my milk finally dried up once I started working, and I could not pump sufficiently.

Because I had minored in elementary education, I had enough credits to get a substitute teacher's license. For the next three years, until Garth was born, I did substitute teaching in some of the toughest schools in Brooklyn and lower Manhattan. Teachers with seniority could transfer to schools in "better" (i.e., white, middle-class) neighborhoods, so the schools in Bedford Stuyvesant, the Lower East Side, and other poor areas often had teacher shortages. The first day I appeared to substitute teach in a school in the shadow of the Brooklyn Bridge (many years before the area was gentrified), wearing a hat and white gloves as was required in 1961, I was offered a job as a full time substitute. Apparently, if you were a warm body and breathing, they would hire you because the school only received payment from the state for covered classrooms. The children would be divided and sent into other classrooms if they couldn't find a substitute for the day. I didn't know what I was doing, never having had a classroom internship, and didn't want to work full-time, so I rejected the offer. I usually worked two or three days each week, receiving the munificent salary of $25/day.

We stayed in the Park Slope apartment for two months, never unpacking our boxes. We had to walk through the owner's living room to take the staircase to our little attic apartment. We moved to a nice apartment in the Fort Greene area on Washington Street just a half block from Nostrand Avenue, which was the northern boundary of Bedford Stuyvesant, then a poor black community.

I got a substitute teaching job in an innovative program preventing delinquency by identifying third and fourth-graders early. The two classes had three teachers, with home visits and lunch in their classroom, so that they wouldn't get into lunchroom fights. Liz Murra, the teacher I worked with, was a remarkable woman who knew how to give these troubled children love and discipline. I learned she was probably a lesbian, living with a beautiful young woman. When I told Mel about her situation, he immediately set up a date with his male friend for her roommate. Being lesbian was in the closet then, and she could not refuse. This was an example of his nature, finding weaknesses or vulnerability in others and using it for his own gratification and sense of power.

Soon I was hired as a "permanent substitute" in another school just around the corner from our apartment, with the same program where I would be the fourth-grade teacher. The principal did not support the program and would not allow the children to eat in the classrooms, claiming that it would attract vermin. He also did not want me to make home visits because he cautioned me, "I once went on a home visit with the welfare worker because this mother claimed more kids than were living with her. We got chased down the stairs by her boyfriend with a knife." Well of course they weren't welcomed, as they were trying to take away some of the mother's welfare check. I decided I would make visits and visit every child's home. The kids loved it! They saw me talking to their mothers (mostly single parents.)

The kids were all Puerto Rican or African American. My eyes were opened to the horrific conditions in which they lived and their amazing resiliency in the face of their conditions. One mother lived in a three-room apartment with seven kids. She had no living room, so I spoke to her sitting on the edge of her bed and noticed a gin bottle under the bed. I thought I'd be slugging gin if I were in her situation.

In front of their kids, a few parents gave me permission to swat them if they got out of hand. Of course, I wouldn't, but it was a tremendous sign of trust in a white woman teacher, and now the kids saw that their parents and I were a team, so that they couldn't play off one against the other. One home I entered was darkened in the middle of the day. An infant was propped up on pillows on the big bed in the middle of the living room, with the TV turned on. As I spoke to the mother, her eyes seemed dazed, and she seemed out of it. I was convinced she was on drugs.

One tall, skinny, quiet girl always came late to class, usually fifteen or twenty minutes after the bell. When I visited her home, I learned they had no clock in the house. Amazingly, this ten-year-old child would get herself up, dress, and go to school every day. I then realized that these children's problems were so much more than what a teacher could fix.

In my other substitute gigs, I had seen different school environments. In some, the halls were eerily quiet, and the kids were forced to sit rigidly at their seats with their hands clenched on their desks. Other schools were so *laissez-faire* that kids ran wildly in the halls, and teachers seemed to have little control. These vivid experiences were etched in my memory and led me to conclude that I couldn't do much to help individual children when facing such massive environmental challenges. It began my quest to make change at the structural rather than the individual level.

At Christmas break, Mel had me helping him with his artistic endeavor, mixing paints for him. After the break ended, he cajoled me not to go back, just as he had in Florida. I kept calling in sick, so after about ten days, I was fired. Again, I had enjoyed and gotten satisfaction from this job, but once more, he manipulated me into losing my sense of self to be a "good wife."

Soon we had to move again, and Mel found us an apartment on East 10th Street between Avenues B and C, in what was then the Puerto Rican part of the East Village. The walk-through apartment was a converted storefront. Mel planned to use the front room as his studio and gallery, and we'd live in the kitchen and bedroom in the rear. He built a loft sleeping platform in the rear room, and he and his friend Miltie embarked on renovations. They took down the plaster and exposed the beautiful brick wall behind it in the front room. But we had an infant, and there was probably lead paint dust all over the house. By now, Lorena was crawling and starting to walk. Amazingly all this did not damage her. In my ignorance, I had no idea of the danger.

I think I was probably suffering from post partum depression or emotional abuse. I wasn't bathing, wearing flip-flops, no underwear, and unironed old dresses. I must have been washing diapers by hand, as we had no washer, dryer, or money for the launderette. Neither of us was working, although this may have been when he and Milty embarked on a short-lived career as home decorators doing painting and plastering. Like his other ventures, that didn't last long. We were collecting bottles for deposit, and I would buy a can of sausage for protein with the nickels. My milk had dried up because I couldn't pump while teaching. One day during lunchtime, I had tried using my manual pump in a tiny, dark, filthy school toilet. If I didn't pump, I would drip milk on my blouse, and by the time I returned home, I would be in agony.

After Lorena was a few months old and could tolerate cow's milk, I relied on powdered milk, which was much cheaper than fresh. I rarely did any subbing now, so I'd spend my day walking around town with Lorena in a stroller, through Tompkins Square Park, sometimes to St. Mark's Place, and even down to the City Hall area, all in my flip flops. In the summer afternoon, the adults on our street would turn on the fire plugs for the kids to play in the spray. At night there was loud music, noise, and sometimes gang fights, but no one ever bothered us. We were a part of the neighborhood. With my long hair and dirty feet and Mel in old clothes and greasy hair, we didn't look like wealthy white tourists.

Around this time, Mel discovered marijuana and would buy a kilo and sell small $5 bags. He'd invite friends to parties to sample it and often smoked up the profits. When money and food ran low, we'd take the subway to his mother's house, and he'd raid her pantry for lots of groceries and canned goods. We went to a supermarket a couple of times, and he gave them a bad check. Somehow he had found a checkbook and was using that. Once, he had me do it. I didn't want to, but I was so under his control and emotionally wrecked that I did whatever he said. I had a massive load of groceries in the shopping cart. I went to the manager and presented the check for payment. He said, "You look like an honest person," and accepted my check. I was so ashamed and devastated that I never did it again and have never forgotten that day nor the man whose faith in the goodness of people was probably destroyed because he had trusted me. It's something on my conscience that I still live with.

Once, we were invited to the country home of the parents of Jack, a friend of ours. A large group of couples were up for the weekend and had a big party. We were all stoned on pot. The room was dark, the music pounding, and the sweet smell of incense and marijuana filled the air. People, in silhouettes, were dancing. I looked across the room and had a vision of Mel, with his little Vandyke beard beating his bongos, looking like the devil. I decided then to leave him. He left that night, and I spent hours confiding in Jack and another friend.

The following day, I ran through the meadow barefoot, the breeze in my long hair. I felt free! That didn't last long. Mel returned and put a guilt trip on me about how our baby needed both parents. He begged me to take him back, and of course I did. I couldn't get away. When

Jack called the next week to find out how I was doing, Mel didn't let me speak to him. He isolated me further from any friends. We spent much time up in the loft smoking pot. That was my escape from thinking about who I had become.

Once again, we had to move because we were behind in our rent. This time we moved to an apartment on West Broadway, on the Lower East Side, owned by an Orthodox Jewish man. When I was pregnant, Mel frequently went out to a new college on Long Island, Stony Brook, and met a girl named Ellen. He had suggested we have an open marriage, as he said he had lied to me about Mona and had never had a chance to sleep with any other woman. What was the truth about Mona? I'll never know. I said I didn't want that; I believed in being loyal and faithful to one man. He said he would do it anyway, and I had no choice in the matter. He brought Ellen to our apartment, where he slept with her in the front room while I slept in the bedroom with Lorena. There was no depth to my humiliation, and I allowed it. Only years later did I understand that I was one of those emotionally abused women I read about.

One day Mel had me, with Lorena in her stroller, descend the stairs at the 8th Street subway station for the A train. We were going to the apartment of his drug connection up in Harlem. He was a tall, broad, tough-looking Black guy who sold heroin and had just been released from jail. I was terrified, as I had to stay in his apartment with some other men while he and Mel went someplace to purchase the pot. Mel had the money. I had no idea if he'd be robbed or killed, and I was afraid I would be raped. I focused on caring for my baby; nothing happened except my terror. On the way back, he had me put the kilo of pot he had purchased in the stroller because, he said, the cops would never suspect it there. Of course, if we had been arrested, I would have gone to jail, and he probably would have denied knowing anything about it. So many women have been imprisoned for situations like this while their boyfriends go free. Again, I just went along with what he wanted me to do. We took the A train back to the Village from

Harlem, getting back to our now quiet street without incident at about three in the morning.

A few years earlier, we had become friends with Paddy and Ed, a poet and painter, and Paddy's sister Heather and her partner. They had apartments over a funeral parlor on the Flatbush extension, just where the Brooklyn Bridge incline began. Paddy's first partner, Wally, who became psychotic, had talked about his guru in California. Mel was intrigued. So now, in 1962, Mel decided we should move to San Francisco so he could study with this guru. He bought an old car for about $80, and we would load up our things and head west. Before we left, Mel expressed his rage at Orthodox Jews like our landlord by painting horrid vulgar words all over the walls in black paint. As a child, he had been sent to cheder, the religious school for pious Jewish boys. I have no idea what kind of abuse he suffered there or at the hands of his Orthodox father.

So, we started our journey. There were no seat belts then, so Lorena, now one and a half years old, was usually playing on the floor in front of my seat. We had piled some of my few remaining treasured possessions on top of the car; my college books with notes in them, a beautiful large silver-plated Persian tray we had used as a side table with its folding wooden legs, and a statue of a wooden elongated seated Buddha. We believed Paddy and Ed had moved to Charlottesville, Virginia (they actually moved to Charlotte, NC), so instead of heading west on the new Interstate 90 from NY, we headed south. Of course, we couldn't find them, and I thought that instead of backtracking, why not just take Interstate 80 west? Bad idea. It was an older, two-lane road that took us over the Alleghenies, and the old car couldn't make the hills. Mel insisted I throw away all my stuff from the top of the vehicle, which added to our weight. I remember sadly gazing at them all strewn on the side of the road

Another piece of my identity was thrown away.

The radiator overheated, spewing steam, and eventually, the motor conked out. We tried to get it fixed, but it was no use. We wired my parents, who sent us money to buy another used car. On we trudged. I remember one night we camped (without equipment—just a tarp) somewhere in Oklahoma. It was bleak and dusty. That's one state I've never returned to.

We continued, both out of sorts, until we got to the old, famous Route 66 through New Mexico and Nevada. When we finally got to Needles, in the Mojave Desert, the car once again overheated. Once again, I wired my parents, but they refused to help us any further. I suggested to Mel that we stay in this town for a while and work until we could make enough money to replace the radiator. No, Mel insisted; he didn't want to be stuck in this place. I think we finally got some money from his mother and completed our journey up the coast of California to San Francisco.

Our destination was the commune where my old camp buddy, Ellen, lived. She had graduated from the High School for Performing Arts, had a gorgeous, sweet soprano voice and made her living singing old Appalachian folk songs, accompanying herself on her guitar. Ellen shared a little house with several other young people in the Fillmore neighborhood (before gentrification.) The night we got there, exhausted from a 12-day grueling journey, Mel announced that the trip had been so hard for him that he had to return to New York! Although we had no money, he managed to pay for airfare, probably using another forged check and leaving me alone with our baby. Only much later did I learn he had returned to his girlfriend.

My friend Ellen knew an older woman with a spare bedroom. She was kind enough to take me in, and I immediately started feeling that a weight had been lifted from me. I felt free, like I had that time a year before, as I ran down the hilly street to the bus. I finally had control over my life; I had a place to live and got a teller job at Wells Fargo Bank. The woman I lived with had a friend, and he and I had started to date.

One night, while I was out, Mel called, and the woman, who I think was jealous, told him I was out with a man. He was furious, even though he left me to return to his girlfriend. He immediately took a plane out and confronted me. I didn't want to return to him, but he plied me with pot, again putting a guilt trip on me, talking on and on for hours until my head spun. I didn't know who I was anymore, and the thought that ran through my head in my pot daze was "past, present, future remembered." For some reason, it scared me.

So, Lorena and I returned to New York with him. I believed I was losing my mind but was sane enough to tell myself I had to act like I was normal. In those days, a husband could admit his wife to an insane asylum. What kept me going was my fear of losing not only my freedom but my daughter. We still had no money or any place to live, so Mel arranged for us to live in his mother's house, along with his four siblings. His old room upstairs was no longer available, having been added to the tenants' apartment.

I started substitute teaching again, still convinced I was going crazy but determined to act sane. His mother babysat Lorena, and I have no idea what Mel was doing while I worked. His *bubby*, an old white-haired woman in layers of old clothes, who spoke only Yiddish, was often seated at the kitchen table. Having obtained throw-away rotting fruit from the outdoor pushcarts on Sutter Avenue, she'd sit there peeling fruit, cutting out the rotten parts, and stewing it all in a big pot. The smell of cooked apples, peaches, or whatever wafted through the room, imparting a delicious aroma.

We had left for the west in November 1962; by the spring of 1963 we had enough money to rent our apartment. This time we moved into a loft that had previously been used as a small garment factory on the first floor of a loft building on Stanton and Clinton Streets on the Lower East Side. The building was hidden in a courtyard behind an apartment house, so you had to walk through the hallway of the first building to get to our building.

Mel was busy fixing up the loft. First, he purchased sheets of plywood to cover the old splintered and chipped floor. Then we bought a used claw leg bathtub and kitchen appliances. Fortunately, the loft already had plumbing and electric wiring. Above us lived Stan, a sculptor, and above him, a middle-aged gay couple. I remember a little playground I could see from one of our windows where I'd take Lorena and put her on the baby swings.

I was working, and Mel spent our money buying paints, canvasses, and pot. We'd often have big parties at the loft. One friend was working in a lab where they started manufacturing LSD. He said he had tried it and had such a bad trip that months later, he still suffered from flashbacks. The poet Ed was often there, drinking pure alcohol, which was cheaper than vodka. Once, I thought he would drop dead— his face turned bright red, and his eyes teared. Fortunately, he survived, but those were the days when drugs and casual sex began to become the scene. I had also been smoking pot, but while, in the beginning, I had some benign experiences, I was now becoming more paranoid with use. Once, Mel suggested we try some heroin. I refused, thinking if I was so affected by the pot and my friend had such a bad trip on LSD, what could happen to me if I ever tried any other drugs? That decision may have saved my life.

I immediately found a permanent substitute job teaching fifth grade in a huge old elementary school building in the middle of a housing project on Houston Street and Avenue D. All the kids were Black or Hispanic. I had a class of thirty-one kids, of whom probably ten had ADD (Attention Deficit Disorder), but we had no such diagnosis then, nor any teacher's aides. I had a hard time controlling the kids. I liked them but was warned by other teachers, "Don't smile until Thanksgiving." I tried some innovative techniques. When we were studying Columbus' journey to the New World, I wanted to teach them about the need for spices, which was the reason for his journey. I brought an apple to class, studded it with cloves, and left it in the closet to show them how spices would preserve food. The problem was that some kids would sneak into the closet, take a clove, and eat it. The apple rotted. The experiment failed.

The teachers in the lounge used to speak so negatively, with such hostility and condescension—and racism--about the parents, I couldn't bear listening to them. The school was huge, with twelve classes in each grade. I had class 5-10. Children were assigned to class sections according to ability. Funny thing, 5-1 had the lightest complexioned kids, and 5-12 had the very darkest!

I had to select readers for the class at the beginning of the school year. They were still at the 4th-grade reading level, but those books were old and dirty. I thought it would be such a negative message to distribute those books to them on the first day of class. I entered the storage room and found brand-new 5th-grade readers. True, they were all about white pioneer children in the West. That would have no relevance for these kids, but at least they were clean and new.

In the first week of November, the principal entered my room. "Children, put your readers on your desks." I had no idea what was going on. He had never spoken to me about this. When they had done so, he ordered, "Now, the first child in each row, collect those books and bring them to the front of the room." He instructed those children to take the books and follow him out of the room. On his way out, he turned to address me, "These books are for 5-1, not your class." That was the end of any semblance of control I had over the class. I had been humiliated in front of them. I had no authority. They were not as important as the other kids. Of course, they acted out terribly after that. He and that school led to my decision never to teach in public schools again. That happened soon enough. I was pregnant again, due in June, so when winter break came, I resigned. Teachers still couldn't work once they looked pregnant.

That fall, after we had moved in and I started working, I began to feel better about myself, taking dance and pottery classes at the Henry St. Settlement. I hadn't planned to have a child then, but we were not using birth control. When I started to show, I dropped both classes. I thought I was bummed out by this second pregnancy when my life with Mel was so chaotic. But I recently found an old piece of composition paper on which I had written these words when I first thought I might be pregnant. I'm surprised at my reaction. I wrote:

".... my mind and body feel right, a good feeling, as I felt when carrying Lorena. It's like all the anxieties melt away—what to do with your life, what to be, how to create. Those things fade away because something inside is just right –just what a woman needs."

Now I cringe at that last sentence—was I so locked into that culture of what women need?

When I returned home after the last day before winter break, I entered the loft and shut the door. I was so relieved not to be teaching in that school any longer and relished the months I'd have at home before my second child would arrive. Although we were still short of money, and although we were Jewish, Mel had splurged on a huge Christmas tree, almost touching the high ceiling. The loft was filled with the pungent scent of pine. At that moment, Mel announced he was moving out. He now had another girlfriend. I was astounded. Here I was pregnant, again at my most vulnerable, but after the last time I had tried to leave and almost fell apart, I had made a pact with myself. I didn't believe I would have the mental strength to try to leave him again, but if he ever decided to leave me, I wouldn't stop him! I think he was surprised that I didn't beg him to stay.

The plan was that we would "sell" the loft. Of course, we didn't own it, but the custom was that if a new renter wanted it, they would pay an agreed-upon fee for first dibs with the landlord and all the appliances we had acquired. Never did Mel offer to support me, nor did I expect or demand it (I never demanded anything of him.) Before we left the loft, one day, he sexually abused me. I had never had an orgasm with him, and he took this as a threat to his pride. At some level, I withheld, fearing that if he could give me an orgasm, I'd be totally in his power. On New Year's Eve, he left me alone with Lorena while he went to a party with his new girlfriend, Hetha.

Soon after, he moved out to live with her; I had no money, so in his "beneficence," he said I could keep what we sold the loft furnishings for, and it would support me until after the baby was born, But now where was I to go? I had been cut off from my friends and was ashamed to return to my parents, where I would have to acknowledge they had been right all that time. I wasn't even sure if they would be willing to take me in.

One day, when I stopped at Stanley's Bar on Ave B and 12th St., I met a friendly young man named Frank. He had been in Mexico, where he had tried mescaline and subsequently spent time in a psychiatric ward. He had just gotten out. We talked, and after a while, I invited him to the loft. When he heard about my predicament, he graciously offered to let me stay at his apartment until after the baby was born. He lived nearby in another tenement building. I sold the loft furnishings for $700 and moved into his three-room walk-up apartment. As we were moving in, two little girls, who lived in the building, were running up the stairs to his apartment. He told them they couldn't visit him anymore.

As my delivery day was getting closer, I spent more time sleeping. He'd often be in the living room playing his saxophone, sometimes watching Lorena for me so I could nap undisturbed. One day I had a disturbing premonition. I quietly entered the living room and found him abusing my not-yet-three-year-old child. I finally realized he was a pedophile! I immediately packed our things and Lorena, and called Mel, telling him he'd have to take us in. I grabbed a cab to the apartment he was sharing with Hetha. A couple of days later, I went into labor and begged Mel to stay with me during the delivery of our child. He refused, but he and Hetha cared for Lorena while I was in the hospital.

I was back at Beth El Hospital, but this time as a clinic patient. The nurses were not nearly as nice as they had been on my first visit.

Because of my Lamaze training, I knew when I was ready to deliver and begged the nurse to get the attending doctor. It was the middle of the night, and she didn't want to "disturb his sleep." Finally, when she saw the head start to crown, she got him, and they rushed me to the delivery room while I was already beginning to push, breathing as I had been taught. Again, I wanted no medications, and it was a long and painful delivery as Garth was a lot larger than Lorena had been, weighing 8 lb. 6 oz at birth. Still, the moment he was born, I was so happy all was forgiven, although the nurse never even smiled at us.

While I was in the hospital, Mel had "helpfully" rented an apartment for me on the corner of 6th Street and Second Avenue. Including our stay in California and his mother's home, this would be the twelfth and last move of my six-year marriage. He rented it in his name and had a key to it. It was a dump, on the first floor over a Chinese restaurant, with smells of cooking oil and spices wafting into the apartment along with visiting roaches. Not only was there no lock to the front door of the building, but my toilet was in the hall. When the New York New Tenement Laws were passed in the early 1900s, all buildings were required to have indoor toilets. On a floor with four apartments, they were required to have two toilets in the hall that renters could share. That had changed, so now two of the apartments had inside toilets while I and another tenant on the floor had our very own toilet in the hall, with a lock. This was very common in the old buildings in the West and East Villages in those days. The bathtub was in the kitchen with a white porcelain cover that could be used as a counter when the tub was not in use. There was no way I would use that toilet in the hall at night, so I would pee in the tub and turn the faucet on to wash it down the drain.

Lorena slept on a mattress on the floor and Garth in a crib, but he was colicky, and I often walked the floor and rocked him at night. One night I heard a sound behind the wall and noticed a hole. I was convinced it was a rat. I was petrified. Fortunately, I had some friends living in an apartment a few flights up. I grabbed both kids and knocked on their door. The husband proceeded to get some heavy- duty steel wool and filled the hole. That seemed to help, as I never heard those sounds again.

We had an agreement that Mel would name our son, so even though he had walked out on me and wasn't supporting us, I foolishly honored our agreement. The name on the birth certificate is Garcia Whitman Brandwein, after Garcia Lorca and Walt Whitman. Later I changed his name to Garth Whitman, which appears on all his school records. Garth was born in late April, two days before my birthday. I always said he was my best birthday present!

A couple of months later, Mel announced that he had bought an old VW wagon, and they were going to California to find his guru. (I previously described this in the prologue.) He wanted me and the children to come with them. Once he was out of my physical space, the fog in my head had slowly lifted, and I could think clearly again. I began to have a sense of self, of agency. I was adamant about not joining them. O.K., he said, then I'll take Lorena, and we'll have joint custody. After six months, I'll bring her back for your six months. Sure! No way did I believe him. First, I didn't even know where they were going, and second, if he did bring her back, he'd try to manipulate me by trying to convince me that Lorena thought of Hetha as her mother (he was already getting her to call her Mommy) and wouldn't I want what was best for her? I refused to go and did not want him to take her with them.

PART II
A New Life

CHAPTER 5

Seattle

I couldn't believe I had done it! I had outwitted Mel and gotten away with the kids. It was a matter of survival. He had tried to take Lorena—he didn't care about Garth, who was just an infant, but he had a real thing about Lorena. He used to have her bounce on his pelvis when he was lying down playing "horsey." Once, he told me that when she was twelve, he would be the first man to "break her in." He had threatened to have the court declare me an unfit mother. No way was I going to give up my children, especially not to a pot-smoking, lying con man. That's what I realized he was. He would always do whatever was good for him. He thought nothing of lying and hurting others. He had to dominate others. And when he wanted to, he could be oh-so-charming.

Many years later, I realized he fit the description of a sociopath. I dreaded to think what he would have done to me if he had found us. I was determined not to let my mind dwell on Mel or even dream of him, and I didn't. I still had this irrational fear that he had mental power over me, and if I thought about him, he would find us.

I had met Mel when I was just fourteen, and I was rebelling against my family. By fifteen, we were doing some heavy petting, and I was no longer a virgin at sixteen. After four years, we married, had two children, and separated after six years. In those ten years, from fourteen to twenty-four, my brain and personality were still developing, but I had been deprived, or deprived myself, of the normal ways girls learn how to relate to boys. I did have a crush on Marty, the writer, in high school, and many years later, he told me he had really liked me, but we were both too shy to know how to express our feelings. I went out once with another boy, but my mother said he was too old for me and feared he would take advantage of me—how ironic. I was two years ahead of myself in school, and it was important in the 1950s to have a boyfriend, even if what we did was a secret. He would lie about so many things that I never knew the truth and could never fully trust him. I loved him—or thought I did and was ambivalent about my feelings from the start. He hurt me terribly and destroyed my ego and self-confidence, and years later, I learned a name for what was happening—I had been emotionally abused. When I finally left him, I resolved that I would have to protect myself. I would be my own person. That first primary relationship taught me men could not be trusted. I feared I would lose myself if I allowed myself to get too close in a relationship.

When I finally fled New York, my parents were on vacation. I borrowed a few hundred dollars from my Aunt Lil and Uncle Herb, who didn't pry. I told no one that I was leaving or where I was going. Only my lawyer knew. He advised me to use one incorrect digit when giving my social security number so Mel couldn't track me. Eventually, I could contact Social Security and tell them my error, getting my contributions back into my correct account.

Mel was incensed when he found I had left. He questioned my parents, but they didn't know my whereabouts at the time. They later told me he never asked how the children were and if we were all right. He was convinced I had fled to Denver, where I had another aunt and uncle. Poor Aunt Gertie and Uncle Harold! They were hauled into the police station and questioned. Of course, they, too, knew nothing, but I think it was the most exciting experience in their lives!

I finally landed in Seattle after a difficult but liberating six-hour flight and hours more before on the bus and train to the airport. I didn't know a soul. I had a three-year-old and a four-month-old, one suitcase, and $200. I got a cheap hotel room, as I recounted in the Prologue. I paid for it and got the kids to the room. I was still nursing Garth but had to find food for Lorena and me. Downstairs and across the street, I found a natural foods store and bought a can of soy meat. We ate that. Then I went to the public phone booth on the corner (they still had those) and looked in the Yellow Pages for babysitters. To my delight, they had listed those licensed by the city.

I chose a lady in the Wallingford neighborhood. The following day, I took the bus there, deposited the kids with Mrs. Gates, and looked for a waitress job, although I had never waited tables before. I needed money coming in immediately and figured that would bring some in while I looked for other work. I also found a furnished three-room apartment in Wallingford, way before it was hip, for only $70/month. I was lucky because, in those days, you could find cheap apartments. If it were now, we would probably have landed in a homeless shelter. It was a lower-middle-class, respectable neighborhood not far from the university. I had a judge inside my head (my superego?) who, I feared, would take my kids unless I kept to the straight and narrow. No pot, no hanging out with beatniks and hippies, no men, no living on a cool houseboat, just work, take care of the kids, and cover your tracks so he can't find you. We moved there immediately.

Within a few days, I had found a babysitter, an apartment, and a waitress job. I thought I was in heaven. Instead of the grimy Lower East Side, I had a second-floor airy apartment with a sun porch, a little grassy yard in front, clean streets, and friendly people. Wherever I walked, I saw mountains and water: the Cascades and Lake Washington to the east and Lake Union and the Cascades to the west, beyond which lay Puget Sound. Bus drivers greeted you and said, "Have a good day," when you disembarked.

My lawyer had advised me to apply for welfare. In those days, you could qualify if you were poor and had children. But I didn't want to go on welfare. I feared the government would look into my life and possibly remove my children. I wanted my privacy, which you give up when you go on welfare. For that first month, though, I supplemented my meager income with Dept. of Agriculture supplemental foods.. I went to the distribution center where they gave out powdered milk, a brick of Velveeta-type cheese, rice, some cans of beef (really good), and whatever else surplus foods were available then.

My first job was waitressing at the Mayflower Hotel downtown. The customers were mainly hotel residents, old blue-haired retired school teachers who insisted on fastidious service but who couldn't afford to tip. I wasn't shaving my underarms, and I heard one woman disparage my odor. She was saying something about "those people." I thought to myself, "She has no idea who I am. I'm a college graduate who is Phi Beta Kappa." We made hourly wages if we worked over a half hour. I was on the dinner shift, and we had to clean up after the restaurant closed, which took twenty minutes. I suggested to the manager that after three nights, that would add up to another hour's wages. She wouldn't agree, so with that excuse and my discomfort around the clientele, I quit.

Then I found a job at Dick's Coffee Shop on University Way near the university and a short bus ride from my apartment. Again, I was put on the supper shift, as they knew I wasn't experienced, and breakfast and lunch were busier. The tips weren't much better, as the clientele was mostly faculty and students, but they were much friendlier. I was still using Mrs. Gates as my babysitter until one day

Lorena told me that Mrs. Gates had spanked Garth because he dirtied his diaper right after she had changed it. I wouldn't let anyone hit my baby, so I immediately removed them both from her care and found another sitter.

Walking down University Way from the coffee shop one afternoon, I noticed a "Martha Nishitani Dance Studio" sign on the second floor. I went up and asked her if she could use a modern dance teacher. "I'm a one-woman operation, but the Park Department is starting new programs with specialists in their Recreation Centers. Maybe you can get a job with them." I found the Parks Department headquarters on Dexter Avenue near the Seattle Center and was interviewed by the director. He didn't have any dance instructor jobs, but when he learned I had worked in the Black neighborhoods and housing projects of New York, he offered me a job as the female leader in their Recreation Center at Yesler Terrace. This was a public housing project of low-rise apartments on Yesler Way and 10th Street, on a hill facing Mt. Rainier and the VA hospital to the south. The qualifications for the job were either an education or physical education major, and I had only a minor in education, but they were having difficulties finding anyone willing to work there, so he bent the rules to hire me.

This was great. It paid a lot better than waitressing. My hours would be 2:00 to 10:00 p.m., which meant I could have mornings with the kids. I had been looking for a late shift job, but when I applied at the telephone company, they rejected me. I had done too well on their exam, so they were sure I wouldn't stay long. I had never learned to type well, so, fortunately, I couldn't get a job as a secretary. Now I could place Lorena into the cooperative preschool program that required mothers to volunteer one morning a week. I found a babysitter who would come at 1:30, prepare their dinner, and put them to bed. She would leave at 10:30 when I arrived home.

Ironically, just as I had taken this position, I learned that another job I had applied for had come through. It was a state public assistance worker. The state later started a program to help their workers attend social work school. Again, like the earlier WelMet Camp job I didn't take, that would have led me to social work school. The Yiddish word *bashert* means fate. Maybe I was fated to become a social worker, even having rejected both those opportunities.

I had no car, so I had to take the bus downtown and then change at Third and Union for the bus that stopped right in front of Yesler Terrace. Coming home after ten at night, this was then a pretty sketchy neighborhood, well before the Benaroya Concert Hall was built on that corner. After working and living in the East Village, I wasn't scared--Seattle seemed pretty tame.

My immediate supervisor, Gene Boyd, was a jovial, older, heavy-set, short, red-faced Irishman. He would occasionally drop in to see how we were doing. The male leader was a soft-spoken, tall African American man who probably had a sports background. The third staff member, our assistant, was a young, very thin Chinese American who had Type 1 diabetes. When I started, the little kids were running in and out of the gym, and the teenage boys monopolized the gym at all hours playing basketball. I asked one, "Don't you have homework? Don't you want to prepare for college?"

"We are. The only way we'll get there is with a basketball scholarship."

Here I was, just twenty-four years old. I don't know how I had the nerve to establish my authority, but I did. I was the lead staff person. Somehow, having a role to play allowed me to assert myself. I first established rules that the gym was for elementary school kids until 6:00 p.m. After that, the older kids could use the facility. Then I said Mondays and Wednesdays would be for the boys and Tuesdays and Thursdays for the girls. Friday, we could have co-ed volleyball. I didn't work Saturday mornings so the boys could use the gym then. The other staff backed me up, and it worked. I started working with the girls, some of whom were outstanding athletes.

When the Park Department introduced girls' floor hockey, I read the instruction manual and taught it to the girls. I would transport them to hockey and basketball games with other centers, acting as one of the referees and defending my girls when I thought the other referees were prejudiced against my Black kids. My team won many of their games. Once, I took them to a basketball game up on Queen Anne Hill. If you know Seattle, you know that it is one of the very steep hills. I was now driving a used VW Bug I had bought for $200 and, at the age of twenty-five, had a friend teach me to drive. The five teenage girls who piled into the bug were all big. I knew the car could not get up the hill with all that weight, so I had them get out, and they ran up the hill, where I met them at the top.

I started dance and art classes for the young kids. At Christmas, I took them around the project singing Christmas Carols. We decorated the Christmas tree the Park Dept. had provided, with strings of popcorn and cranberries I brought. I also had them paint, put glitter on the cardboard egg containers I had saved and put little bells inside them. I bought some heavy gold paper, and we cut out strips, pasted them in rings, and connected them in long ribbons of decorations for the tree. I also got the little kids to fold white paper squares and cut designs. Our "snowflakes "decorated the many window panes in front of the building. At Easter, volunteers walked down the hill to the egg distributor and got them to donate about eight dozen eggs. Then I boiled them, and the kids and I had fun decorating the eggs.

I was enjoying myself, being creative, and having the freedom to try out whatever I wanted with these kids. Every year, the Parks Department had a Field Day at Green Lake Park, where all the centers competed in various races. There was also a parade. I decided our center would, for the first time, enter the parade. My idea was a parade of animals. I enlisted the older boys to go down the hill and get large empty cardboard boxes from the appliance store. Then I outlined life-size animals like tigers, lions, and giraffes. The younger kids painted them, and the older boys cut them out and glued sticks in the back to be held in front of each child. It was sensational! We won first prize, and the kids' photo was on the first page of the second section of the next day's newspaper. They were so proud of themselves!

On the evenings, when the teenage girls used the gym, I decided I needed to develop an activity for the boys so that they wouldn't be constantly harassing and teasing the girls. I started "Teen Talkout" in the lobby. This was so popular that both the girls and the boys attended. Our first speaker was a tall Black civic leader soon to become the director of the War on Poverty in Seattle. Another Black speaker introduced a then-novel idea, "Black is Beautiful," and encouraged them to style their hair in afros and wear dashikis. The kids were embarrassed, teasing each other about their kinky hair. Teen Talkout finally failed because of its success.

Next door, also on the housing project grounds, was a settlement house headed by a minister and social worker. Their programs were highly structured, with only a few kids participating in their clubs, led by group workers. When he saw how successful the "Teen Talkout" was, with large numbers flocking to our doors, he started his program the same evening. But he was able to get McDonald's to contribute food. Guess where the kids went? I can still chalk that up to success as I provided more activities for the kids, even if it wasn't at my recreation center.

I lost myself in my job and loved it, but when I got home at night, I was lonely and depressed. I would sit down with graham crackers, peanut butter, and honey and feed my face. In that first year, I gained twenty pounds. I thank whatever gods that be for Basil Pollitt, my lawyer, who arranged for me to correspond with my parents safely. I explained that in the Prologue. Long-distance calls were expensive, so I anxiously looked for the mail. The highlight of my day would be receiving long, newsy letters from my parents.

Lorena Age 5 and Garth Age 2 at the lakefront

In 1965, I had a beloved reconciliation with my family. My sister Gale had married that June, but I was afraid to set foot in New York State. Instead, my parents found a lake house in the Poconos in Pennsylvania that summer and paid our fare to come out. My sister was there with my new brother-in-law, Jay Lurie, and we all had a great time, with the kids really getting to know their grandparents, aunt, and uncle. I had some meaningful talks with my folks. I had always felt that my father had distanced himself from me as I entered puberty. I loved him and yearned for his affection and attention. He then revealed that my mother's best friend, Belle, had been sexually abused as a child and had warned my father not to get too close to me as I approached puberty. Maybe that was why my mother always seemed to come between us. I often thought she was jealous of me, but perhaps she was trying to protect me. We cried, hugged, and developed a much stronger and healthier relationship. I still chuckle at the home video of little Garth in a highchair at that vacation house, eating and throwing spaghetti all over the floor and smearing it on his face.

As an enthusiastic employee, I always wanted to embark on new initiatives suggested by the Park Department. The Department was launching athletic teams for women. I got some mothers together at the Project and suggested a women's basketball team. No, they didn't want that. Instead, they wanted classes to help them raise their children as single mothers. Using my connections from the cooperative preschool, I got a speaker from the College of Education. This was followed by a pediatrician and a few other speakers on topics they selected. Seeing the faces of the mothers, Black, brown, and white, seriously absorbing new ideas gave me great satisfaction. I guess I was becoming a social worker before I realized I was.

The other new initiative was to form an Advisory Board. The Urban League put on a monthly program called Grass Roots Forum, so I asked Ivan King, who organized it, along with Ken Latcholia, director of the Jackson St. Community Council down the hill, to be members. Soon after, Ken, an African-American, was offered a job with the federal government. This was in early 1966, at the height of the civil rights movement, and ambitious, college-educated men like Ken, who hadn't had many opportunities previously, were now in demand. He recommended me for his position. I didn't think I'd have a chance. I thought they would want a back-slapping, cigar-smoking man like Ken. I was wrong. The work I had been doing at Yesler Terrace was widely known. Judge Charles Z. Smith, who let his daughter come to participate in some of our programs, became a strong supporter. When I was interviewed for the position by one of the older board members, she liked me but suggested I wear longer skirts. I took her advice and began wearing my long hair in a bun to look older and more matronly.

Jackson Street Community Council had been started after World War II in the International District, east of downtown Seattle. At the time, it was home to Jews, Chinese Americans, Japanese Americans returning from internment camps, and a smattering of Negroes (as they were called at the time). The purpose was to achieve interracial and intergroup harmony by creating a venue to work together on community issues. At that time, Violet Seider who was at the national office of the United Community Chests, and Councils (predecessor to United Way) came from Washington to help them organize. Much later, she would become my professor at Brandeis and a dear friend.

Over the years, the Asian-American and Jewish populations moved north, and south of the international district, and the Black population moved further east to the Central Area. The international district had become a commercial area, mainly for Asian-American merchants. The Seattle United Way had been funding two Jackson Street Council staff members all these years. Over that time, several neighborhood councils had sprung up in the Black community, and their members were now seeking similar staff support. There was no way the United Way would fund several small community organizations.

At my first meeting with Milton Karr, head of the planning division at United Way, he explained the situation and told me they would like me to reorganize the Jackson St. Council to staff all the small neighborhood organizations. There were Cherry Hill, Madrona, and Leschi associations at the time. I didn't have a clue how to go about this. Milt suggested I ask Professor Florence Ray Stier, who had just come to the University of Washington School of Social Work to start its community organization sequence, to become my consultant. I went to see Florence, and not only did she help me reorganize it into the Central Seattle Community Council, but she recruited me to obtain my Master of Social Work degree and was to become an important mentor and friend to me in the coming years.

Everything seemed to be going so well. I had turned my life around. I was satisfied with my work, I soon would be starting a prestigious new job with a raise in salary, and my kids were doing well. Now two threatening events shook my equilibrium.

Soon after I had started working in the coffee shop, I met a young man named Ted Saunway. He worked in the post office but also took classes at the U. Ted was tall and stocky, with short legs and thick glasses. Maybe because I didn't find him attractive, I wasn't fearful and found him easy to talk to. On our first date, he thoughtfully took the kids and me to the Seattle Center, where we put Lorena on the kiddie rides.

That first Christmas, I bought Lorena a beautiful green velvet dress, Garth a little short pantsuit, and me a beautiful black dress with a chiffon skirt, all at Goodwill. That was where I did most of my clothes and household goods shopping. Ted took us to dinner at the top of the Space Needle. I had never been there before. I thought it was the most elegant place. In addition to a delicious steak, the vegetable was baby curled ferns! Ted and I remained together through my time in Seattle, although he did have a drinking problem. Growing up with my family who were not drinkers, I didn't know what problem drinking was.

Just around the time I was getting ready for my new job, lightning struck. I was pregnant! I had gone to Planned Parenthood soon after

I arrived in Seattle, and they had fitted me with a diaphragm. It either no longer fit correctly or I was using it wrong because it failed me. I was beside myself. Ted offered to marry me, but I knew that would be a big mistake. As long as we didn't live together and I only saw him occasionally, the relationship worked, but I knew with his drinking, temper, and desire to be a composer, being saddled with three children would be a disaster.

He tried to find me help. First, he obtained some big black pills. I have no idea what they were, but in my desperation, I took them, took hot baths, and ran around Green Lake. I didn't miscarry. Then he found an abortionist in Chinatown. Abortion was still illegal in 1965, but I was desperate. I knew I couldn't have another child now, just when my life was coming together. We tried to find his address in an alley in Chinatown and, thankfully, couldn't find him. I even went to my doctor, who said, "I can't perform an abortion, but if you get one, come back, and I'll examine you to ensure it was done properly and repair any damage."

By this time, I had started divorce proceedings. I knew I didn't want to be tied to my husband for the rest of my life. I did keep his name. (by now, I had dropped my alias) because I believed I had enough obstacles as a single mother and would face more if the children had a different name. It would seem that I had never married. Divorce was enough of a stigma then; being an unmarried mother was much worse. Your children were considered illegitimate—"bastards." I had been in Seattle for two years, had met the residency requirement, and Washington State was more liberal about reasons for divorce than many other states. In New York, then, you had to prove adultery or insanity. I had found an attorney with the help of my New York lawyer, so I turned to him. He knew of an abortionist in Mexico and made contact with me. I asked some friends to care for the children for a few days, explaining that my mother was suddenly ill and I had to go to New York.

Then I boarded a plane for Mexico City, Ted helping to pay the costs. I was scared. I had no idea what awaited me, but I knew I couldn't raise another child. A pleasant young man picked me up at the airport and transported me to the home of a middle-aged woman. Several young women were also living there. I think she ran a brothel as she would be familiar with abortionists for her "girls," but I never asked. I didn't want to know. Seeing I had the money for the procedure, the following morning she accompanied me to the doctor's office.

I was at least three or even four months pregnant by this time and needed a D&C. He put me out, and I didn't know if I would live or die; I didn't know if I would wake up; I just knew I had to go through with it. When I awoke, the doctor seemed chagrined, telling me there had been not one but two male fetuses. What a relief! Not one more child but twins, in addition to my two and five years old. It would have been the end of any real life for me. I've never regretted that decision.

The woman, whose name I had forgotten or perhaps didn't want to remember, took me back home and put me to bed. She and the young women were very solicitous and, after two days, said I was ready to go home. She implored me to get right on the plane. Apparently, another American woman she had helped had decided to do some sightseeing while there and climbed a Mexican ruin. She began bleeding, which caused all kinds of difficulties with the authorities. I promised, and the next day she gave me a little parting gift, a leather purse I kept for many years.

Now, I could focus on the divorce, but I was terrified. My attorney had found Mel's address in California, where he now lived. We used my attorney's address instead of my own, but Mel would know I was in Seattle once the papers were served. I was in a state of constant anxiety. I'd come home at 10:30 p.m. from the Center, not knowing if I would still find my children there. I fantasized that he had come and whisked them away. Once I saw the back of a man in the street and feared it was he. As I got closer, I realized this guy was much taller and broader. I had made a new life but realized I was still mentally locked into what I perceived as his power.

Mel did send me a letter through my attorney. This was his first and last letter—never a birthday card or letter through my parents asking how his kids were. If he couldn't control me, he didn't give a shit about the children he had fathered. The letter was a rambling stream of consciousness with allusions to Christianity, Buddhism, Hinduism, and New Age nonsense. He also said they were no longer his children as I had ruined them and was " the establishment's running dog." I kept that letter for a long time in case I needed proof of his instability.

I was anxious the day of the court proceedings. If he did appear, I didn't know what kind of scene he might make or how charming he would act. He never showed. My attorney had added a child support order. I felt it wasn't necessary, as he hadn't ever supported the children, but he convinced me that if my husband did not pay what was ordered, that could be held against him. My attorney had represented radicals, and the judge seemed prejudiced against him. In full court, he said, in a disparaging tone, "Don't you know you can't include a child support order in the divorce agreement when the other party is out of state? It has to be a separate document."

I was embarrassed for my lawyer, who had been humiliated by the judge. We retired to a chamber, and he wanted to write a new document. At that point, I said NO. I knew he wouldn't pay or would try using it to manipulate me. By now, I knew other divorced women who never knew when or how much they would get each month, keeping them at the mercy of their ex-husbands, who kept them on a financial string. I was working in my new job that was paying a decent salary. The court clerk who asked about my salary expressed surprise, as most women coming before her were waitresses or secretaries earning much less. I might not have enough to buy clothes or go out to dinner, but I could support myself and my children without having more contact with their father. There was no support order or right to visitation in the divorce document. The divorce went through. I never heard from him again.

My new job required night meetings, so I constantly juggled daytime and evening babysitters. For a while, I had a neighbor watch the kids. Lorena had started kindergarten, but Garth needed full-time care, so eventually, I got him into the Mt. Zion Preschool. He was one of the few white children there. I also decided to move to the Central Area closer to my job. Prof Stier advised against it, talking about professional boundaries. She said, "It's not a good idea. You shouldn't live in the same area where your clients live." I disagreed. I thought that being part of the community would be an advantage for a community organization job, unlike a clinical one. These people were not my clients. I considered them participants in mutual civic efforts.

I found a small two-bedroom bungalow to rent in the Leschi neighborhood on South Jackson St., just above Lake Washington. It was an integrated, middle-class neighborhood. In the early 1960s, liberal white families moved back to re-integrate the area. Our house was on the corner with the woods across the street. Down the hill on Lake Washington Drive was a playground where I took the kids on the weekends.

We had a big front yard on a corner lot with a cherry tree, but between the birds and neighborhood kids, I never got to eat one cherry. I learned to mow my lawn, and rake the leaves in the fall. The living room had a real fireplace on one wall, and the opposite wall had a large picture window overlooking Lake Washington and the bridge to Mercer Island. Beyond that was majestic Mt Rainier, often sheathed in clouds with its snow-capped peak rising as if to heaven. On moonlit nights I was thrilled when the moon illuminated that snowy peak.

At the community council, I had a great board of involved citizens, including Carol Richman, a very savvy volunteer with a political science background who lived in Madrona, the neighborhood north of Leschi, along the west shore of Lake Washington. She was a trusted advisor. Another member whose advice I valued was Mr. Derry. A middle-aged African-American man who had a city job, he gave me wise counsel.

"The only thing in politics more important than money is numbers." Congresspeople, he said, will vote the right way even if it's not the party line if they believe enough of their constituency is mobilized. The bosses will give them a pass in those circumstances. He asked rhetorically,

"What's the most important job for politicians?" and answered his question,

"Getting elected. What's the second most important job? Getting re-elected." I've never forgotten that, and I would repeat those words to my policy students when they are engaged in political advocacy in later years.

Mrs. Ponder was an elegant, tall, well-dressed Black woman who was a Republican. I was shocked until she explained how in the old days, the Republicans were the party of Lincoln and the Democrats in the South, even today, were protecting segregation. Bob Dean, a white engineer at Boeing, was the president.

One man, a Japanese American, was vice president and often boasted about his close connection to Senator Jackson, our senior senator. He abused his office by using our stationery for non-council business. I decided that he should not serve another term on the board. I was advised against it because of his presumed power. I thought he was telling us how much influence he has with the Senator. He's probably telling the Senator how much influence he has in the community. What power will he have if he is no longer on our board? We didn't extend his term and never heard from him again. We even had Governor Evans as our guest speaker at our annual dinner that year.

Mr. Powell Barnet, another board member, was an elderly gentleman whose family came from eastern Washington. Once, I asked them how a Black family had settled there. He gave me a history lesson I had never learned in school. He said there were iron mines, and the European workers were striking. The owners came down South and recruited Black workers to break the strike. They had no idea of the circumstances. This gave me insight into how the owners of factories and mines used divide-and-conquer to pit ethnic groups of workers against each other.

Another Japanese American board member, Don Kazama, became a good friend and advisor. He was active in the Japanese American Citizens' League, advocating for reparations for their World War II internments. Here I was, twenty-six years old, the Executive Director of a social service agency, and I was learning American history and about discrimination firsthand from those who had experienced it.

I was becoming part of the neighborhood and had good, supportive neighbors. Mrs. Gerber, a wealthy woman and art collector who had built a large home in the woods up the street, would invite me and the children to come and swim in her pool. Two members of the Leschi Council, who were my neighbors, volunteered to paint my little house after I purchased it from my landlord.

One of the first tasks I gave myself at the new job was to organize additional neighborhood councils. With the help of board members who knew people in those neighborhoods, I quickly organized the Harrison, Mt. Baker, and Montlake communities.

During Thanksgiving weekend in 1967, I saw an article in the newspaper with a simulated photo showing a proposed multilane, limited-access highway down Empire Way, with spaghetti-like connections, with a third bridge crossing Lake Washington. I knew it would be a disaster. This proposed R. H. Thompson Expressway would cut off the central area from the "gold coast," those wealthier neighborhoods along the lakefront. In many large cities, highways like these had ghettoized people experiencing poverty, usually minority communities with a wall of eight or 10-lane traffic.

Moreover, building a third bridge over the lake would destroy the Mt. Baker community—an integrated working-class community. The neighborhood public school immediately to the south of the bridge would have to be destroyed, or the noise and sound pollution would harm the children. All this so that suburban commuters from wealthy Mercer Island to the east could save time getting to work.

I was incensed and, on Monday, began to organize in collaboration with other groups who were also concerned. We had a fantastic coalition of our neighborhood councils, which were situated along the proposed highway route, as well as the Municipal League, and the American Institute of Architects. Our architect and attorney friends would testify whenever the government officials claimed the councils were parochial. When they claimed the liberal do-gooders didn't know the community, we'd trot out our neighborhood council members.

We had engineers, architects, planners, and other technicians with expertise in traffic flow, lane size, and traffic congestion. However, I became known as the people person, emphasizing what the human costs would be to the residents of our communities. Then we got lucky. The newly formed federal Department of Transportation (DOT) introduced the requirement for ascertaining neighborhood impact. After years of advocacy and months of testimony, the highway was dead! It would be another thirty years before a third bridge, much smaller, was finally built. The R. H. Thompson Expressway was never constructed. Advocacy can make a difference because you never know when some unforeseen event—like the new DOT requirements—will make the difference. You just need to be prepared.

Whenever I visit Seattle and drive through the area, I feel like Jimmy Stewart in "It's a Wonderful Life." What a different place might it have been if I hadn't been there? In truth, many of us saved our city. Change can rarely be attributed to just one person. Later, I wrote a paper using this example to illustrate the importance of coalition building for effective community change.

We organized another exciting collaboration to develop a neighborhood school council. Integration had come to Seattle Public Schools with Black children from the Central Area being bussed to north Seattle schools. Parents were complaining—why did only their children have to ride an hour each way and be far from home? Not only that, but the school busses with their kids parked in the back of the building, which they thought was symbolic, and once inside, the children, although in mixed classes, all ate their lunches at separate tables in the cafeteria. Carol and Bea Hudson spearheaded the fight for local control over Central Area schools. Bea, with her husband Matt, had fought against urban renewal, or as it was popularly called, "Negro removal."

We called for a community meeting, inviting representatives from all stakeholders: our neighborhood councils, the National Association for the Advancement of Colored People (NAACP), the Urban League, and even the Black Student Union and the Black Panthers. I recruited the latter two by meeting them where they suggested, in a greasy joint café on East Cherry Street. I was the only white woman in the place. I guess I passed muster because they attended. That Black Student leader is now a retired King County Councilman.

At this all-day meeting, we went around the room asking each representative to state their goals, which we wrote on taped newsprints around the room. Then, we looked for common themes. We all could agree on local control of the schools and quality education. We decided that each organization would continue to push for its other goals. We contacted the School Board and insisted that we have a community vote on forming a locally run board for our community's schools, similar to what the Brownsville-Crown Heights group had recently started in New York.

The school officials never responded. Then, Carol Richman, in her wisdom, said, "No one ever gives you power. You have to take it. If they don't respond, let's have our own election." With that, we heard from the school board and finally negotiated a locally elected board with limited powers to hire principals in elementary schools.

I was now in my late twenties; my divorce was final, so I had the freedom to figure out what to do with the rest of my life. The university offered a course for women thinking of changing careers with the pretentious title "Decision is Destiny." Each week, we heard from different professors in various fields, including social work. I wanted to get a doctorate in archeology or anthropology but feared it would take too long. I might not be able to get a job supporting my kids in such esoteric fields.

Then Florence Stier urged me to attend social work school and enroll in the community organization sequence. I was pretty negative about social work, but I wanted to learn more to be a better community organizer. I also was considering urban planning and public administration. Dr. Lewin, the Associate Dean of the School of Social Work, convinced me by explaining that of the three, only social work had a set of values, which included self-determination and respect for each client's self-worth, as well as social change for social justice.

So, keeping my full-time job with the community council, in the Fall of 1967, I enrolled as a part-time student at the University of Washington for a Master of Social Work. In the first year, I would take only coursework; in the second, with limited course work and a two-day field placement; in my third year I would have to be a full-time student. I didn't know until the first day of classes that I could only choose the community organization concentration in my second year. I had to choose between casework or group work in the first year. I chose the latter but still had to take a casework course. I chafed at the time, but I learned so much, making me a real social worker.

The other fly in the ointment was the Human Development in the Social Environment class. Why did I have to take that? I wasn't going to work with individuals in therapy. Not only that, but the textbook used in the course was the same one I had used years before in my Education Psychology course at Brooklyn College. I met with Professor Cal Takagi, a small, soft-spoken Japanese American man in his late 30s. He listened to my complaints and then quietly but firmly said, "No, you don't have to take the class, but you don't have to come to the school either. This is a required course for all students." I took the course, learned to love and appreciate him, and years later applied some of the theories I had learned to my first published academic article about single-parent families.

Another problem I faced was that I was not eligible for any of the generous Federal tuition aid grants as a part-time student. To the rescue came the American Association of University Women (AAUW). I had never heard of that organization, but they provided my tuition until I became a full-time student. I still contribute to that fine organization every year.

My first field placement was at "The Fircrest School for Retarded Children," only they weren't children and were not "retarded," but developmentally delayed. I worked with a group of four minimally functioning women who were being deinstitutionalized, helping them to learn how to adjust to the outside world. The field supervisor enjoyed having students because she said they could challenge the system when she couldn't. I was working full-time, attending the master's program part-time, and raising my children alone. I took it as a compliment when my advisor, Rino Patti, commended me for not asking for special treatment. Years later, I realized that institutions need to change to support women with children such as me.

At the start of my final year, I resigned as community council director, living on a $400/month federal grant. I interned at the state capital in Olympia with the Department of Mental Health and Mental Retardation that year. I had an opportunity to visit various state institutions firsthand and was moved by the horrible conditions where people were being warehoused rather than helped. Some were so disabled they were unable to move, some had dementia and were left in a large room with others crying or screaming, and some were minimally disabled but without stimulation. I was also responsible for organizing a statewide conference and working with local officials and volunteers. This experience would be valuable to me in later governmental advocacy efforts.

In those years, federal funds were widely available in the social sciences, and the school paid my way to my first professional conference. The National Conference of Social Welfare which (no longer exists) was having its 1968 annual meeting in San Francisco, and I was going! I arranged for childcare and felt free. It was a glorious week. I heard so many inspiring speakers about civil rights and social justice, attended a few all-night student parties, and even joined a protest against Attorney General Ramsey Clark (a good man, but we thought he wasn't doing enough on the grape boycott or Vietnam, or something). We turned our backs when he spoke—not one of my prouder moments. I loved San Francisco, visiting the Ghirardelli Chocolate Factory, riding the trolleys up and down the steep hills, and enjoying the diversity of the people on the streets. How different from my first brief sojourn in San Francisco!

One of the speakers at the conference was a Bryn Mawr professor named Martin Rein. He was Mel's uncle! After his talk, I went up and introduced myself but beseeched him not to inform Mel. He said they had no contact with him. I had known him and his wife, Micky, when I first met Mel. They were very young and just married. He was then a group worker at the Brownsville Boys Club, and she was getting her social work degree. He was overjoyed to see me and made me promise to visit them. The following year, when I again attended the annual social welfare conference in New York City, I took the train out to Bryn Mawr to their home. Marty had just gotten his degree from a new doctoral program in social welfare at Brandeis University. He urged me to continue my education there and would provide a reference.

In 1968, my sister was spending the summer south of San Francisco, where her husband attended a Stanford summer program. Garth was now five, and Lorena was eight. I took them on a memorable camping trip down Pacific Coast Highway 101. I had no camping gear besides a large blue plastic tarp, rope and tent stakes, sleeping bags, and basic utensils. We camped each night in state parks behind the Oregon dunes, stopping each day to inspect tide pools. We saw starfish, sea lions, and the majestic redwood forest. I saw universes in each tide pool, swarming with life, and in each tree, whose millions of leaves harbored insects, birds, and myriad forms of life. It took us a week to complete the trip, driving only about 200 miles daily, but we finally got there and back safe and sound.

In 1970, I graduated with my MSW and already had a job offer to be Director of the Seattle-King County Youth Commission, but I was considering continuing for my doctorate. My argument with myself was that I was used to being poor. I could continue to be with scholarship aid. If I don't go now, I'll probably get too financially comfortable and won't be likely to give it all up to be poor again. On the other hand, I feared that by having my PhD, I'd be too educated to ever find a man who would want to marry me. When I spoke to my other mentor, Rino Patti, my social policy professor, he said, "Don't worry about it; you're already overeducated for the marriage pool!"

I had also heard Saul Alinsky, the radical Chicago organizer, speak and thought about attending his institute instead of an academic doctoral program. Then Rino showed me an article in *The Nation* about a new welfare rights campaign started by a Columbia social work professor named Richard Cloward and a political science professor at CUNY (the City University of New York) named Frances Fox Piven. They were an example of how being a professor gave you freedom and a platform for doing social justice, organizing, and advocacy.

When I started teaching at Boston University, I got to know Frances; she helped me in selecting the Institute of Policy Studies for my sabbatical, and we worked together with the Woman's Committee of 100 (unsuccessfully) against Clinton's Welfare "reform." For some years, she and Dick had a summer home in Millerton, N.Y., where I occasionally visited them. She has remained a good friend and a role model in fearless advocacy for social justice.

Having decided to get a doctorate, the question was where to go. Only a few social work schools focused on social policy and community organization. Rino advised against attending Columbia. He warned that it was a challenging environment (a snake pit), with students getting caught between feuding instructors and taking over ten years to complete their dissertations. On the other hand, Brandeis had a new community organization focus with faculty like Bob Perlman, Arnie Gurin, Violent Seider, David Austin, and Roland Warren. Warren was a community sociologist, and I had read some of his work. Marty Rein gave me a glowing recommendation, as did my professors at the University of Washington. Finally, I decided to go there when they offered me free tuition and a $400 monthly fellowship.

By now, my sister and her husband had moved to Seattle, and my parents had asked themselves, "What are we doing in Brooklyn when our girls and grandchildren are in Seattle?" So, Dad retired early with his generous New York City pension, and in 1969, they moved there, too. They were enjoying retirement, learning about the city, and making new friends. I never asked them to babysit. I had always tried to be independent and did not call on them for any help, nor did they offer it.

So, after having left my family for the West Coast and having them follow me out, I was now moving back east for what I thought would be only two or three years of residency in the Brandeis doctoral program in Waltham, Massachusetts, just outside of Boston. We arranged for Gale, Jay, and their new baby to live in my little house on Jackson Street, which I had recently purchased from my landlord. They would pay the monthly mortgage, which was only about $75. So I packed up the kids and a few belongings in my new little green Morris Minor, and we went cross country on Interstate 90, camping most of the way.

CHAPTER 6

Cross Country Trek
Boston

That summer, I had surgery for my varicose veins. The doctor said it was a "minor operation." I guess he meant it wasn't life-threatening. He didn't say I had to stay off my feet for at least six weeks. I postponed leaving until mid-August, and even then, all that driving just made new veins pop out. The trip east was fun but challenging. Just me and the kids, "Are we there yet?" from the back of the car. We took our time, making many stops—Wall Drug, the Jewel Caves, the Serpentarium, and Mt. Rushmore, all in South Dakota. We camped most of the way, as we had done the previous year, often in state forests or other out-of-the-way camping areas until we reached the Midwest, where there were no campsites, and we had to stay in motels the last two nights.

It did not seem unsafe then, a woman and two little children camping alone, with just a big blue tarp tied to stakes in the ground. I did have my trusty Swiss army pocket knife under my pillow for all the good it would have done. One night in the wilds of Montana, it was so windy I could barely start a fire to cook up the steak I thought would be delicious; after all, this was ranch country. It was barely edible. Another night in Minnesota, when we went to the latrine, I thought a bear had invaded our campsite. It was a raccoon who was enjoying our leftovers on the table.

Finally, after almost two weeks in my little green Morris Minor, we reached Boston. I called it my "anti-car" because it looked more like a 1940s model but unfortunately also ran like one, unfortunately. If I went over 55 mph, it started shaking. We were headed to the Ruvins' home in Brookline. They were old friends of my parents and had invited me to stay while looking for a place to live. Unexpectedly, however, two of their adult sons had arrived with their families for a stay, so they didn't have much room and were less than hospitable.

The night we arrived, exhausted and hoping for a few days' relaxation, Bea handed me a newspaper folded to the want ads. It was just a week before classes started, and I didn't know how hard it would be to find housing in an area with forty full-time colleges and universities, all starting classes simultaneously! The following day, I began my apartment search. Originally, I had hoped to move to Boston because I prefer cities over suburbs. But I was warned that the Boston schools were awful, so I tried to find something in Brookline, but by late August, nothing was available. So, I started chasing leads all over the area, which I was completely unfamiliar with.

I don't know if you've ever driven in Boston, but you wouldn't want to, at least not then. Drivers seem to take road signs and signals as suggestions only. I had never seen a roundabout before and had trouble negotiating where to get off, often circling and cursing loudly (with the windows closed) several times. Next, only some of the side streets and few of the main avenues were marked. I guess they figured if you d uated, so they referred me to it when they were leaving. I was surprised when I didn't get it. My colleague was shocked that this nice Italian grandmotherly landlady told him, "I would never have a divorced woman under my roof!"

After several days of more frantic searching, I found an apartment in a two-family house on Main Street in Winchester, across from a used car lot. This very WASP town with a small working-class area is about forty-five minutes north of Waltham. The owners, who had the second-floor apartment, were a cop, his wife, and a twelve-year-old daughter. Rents were higher here than in Seattle, and I had to pay $200 monthly out of my $400 stipend.

I had always believed I could live anywhere and, in my democratic spirit, thought I could get along with anyone. Boy, was I wrong! Garth was now entering kindergarten, and Lorena was in third grade. When I went to the school to enroll them, I asked to sign them up for school lunch.

"We have no school lunch program."

"Okay, I'll pack their lunches, and they can eat in school."

"No, you don't understand. We believe mothers should be home to give their children lunch. Our teachers are not paid to mind the students at lunchtime."

This was 1970, but it felt like I was back in the 1950s. I managed an arrangement to pay a neighbor to give my kids lunch, another little chunk of my $400 monthly stipend.

Then Garth came home one day and told me a little Chinese American girl in his class was being bullied, and he was protecting her. Garth was large for his age, blue-eyed, with blond hair and a solid build. None of the kids were about to mess with him.

One day, Lorena used her chalk to make a hopscotch game on the driveway. My landlady was indignant. "This is not Roxbury!" (the Black Boston neighborhood.). One night, I realized I was out of milk and drove down the street to the drive-in dairy. I noticed her peeking through her curtains to see where I was going. There was a back door in the kitchen, behind which were stairs leading to the basement that they used. It had no lock, so I put a chain on the door. Again, the landlady was incensed. I guess she had tried entering the apartment when we weren't home.

The final event that made it imperative to move came after their daughter had offered to babysit. When I returned, Lorena told me that she wanted to play "doctor" with them and tried to have them remove their clothes so she could "examine" them. It was almost Halloween, and I remembered the apartment I liked in Newton. I checked, and it would be available on November 1. It was in the Auburndale neighborhood, had excellent schools, and was only about eight minutes from the Brandeis campus. I got help from some of my fellow students to move our meager belongings to our new second-story apartment with a sunporch on a quiet street just off Commonwealth Avenue, a half mile from the Thruway entrance.

So, finally, after the grueling trip and apartment search, I arrived for my first day at Heller (The Florence Heller School for Advanced Studies in Social Welfare at Brandeis University). Several faculty had social work degrees at the time but were augmented by sociologists, economists, and political scientists. As we introduced ourselves, I heard that most of our cohort's other twenty-five or thirty students had gone to private colleges, many in the Northeast. I was the only one with a public high school and college background, so I was a bit intimidated at first, but I did much better than most of my classmates. New York schools had provided a first-rate education.

Some were coming for their master's and could continue straight on for their PhD. Others, like me, already had a master's degree. I was thirty, as were a few others, but most of my classmates were younger. I was the only single mother with children, but I was to learn there was a token like me in each of the prior two years (Eunice Schatz and Mary Davidson, respectively—and we all became deans of social work schools).

On the first day, I got some excellent advice from one of the advanced students that I clung to when things got rough. "They never drop anyone. If you can stick it out, you'll get through." He had also been a community organizer and cautioned me, "Academics are much worse than anyone in community organizing. They'll stab you in the back, and you'll never even know what happened."

I had been advised to take the planning class with the foremost professor in the field, Robert Morris. He was in his sixties and had just gotten back from a sabbatical. He had been anointed by the former dean, who became the college president, to become dean on his return. But in the class entering in 1969, the radical students had rejected his appointment. Instead, Arnie Gurin was made dean. Morris was probably bitter, and I, coming from my former work as a community organizer, may have been seen as one of the radicals. I didn't think about that, but only that he seemed prejudiced against women. I would make a comment on class, which I thought was brilliant but which he would ignore. A few minutes later, a male student in the back of the room would make the same comment, and Morris would praise him highly. At the end of the semester, I dropped his course.

I had first discovered feminism in Seattle when Ted, whom I met at the coffee shop where I worked, had suggested I read a new book, *The Feminine Mystique* by Betty Friedan. As I read it, the scales fell from my eyes. I wasn't weird for not wanting to be a homemaker. I wasn't crazy for desiring a life beyond being a wife and mother. I was not nuts to think I could do anything boys could and want to compete with them intellectually instead of acting dumb and giggly, the way girls were taught. In New York, just after Garth was born, I had read *The Second Sex* by Simone de Beauvoir, but with everything else going on in my life then, it didn't register as this book did. At the University of Washington, together with a group of women students, we organized an all-day conference, "Sexism and Social Work."

With the women's movement in full force in Boston, I joined a group of young academic and social scientists to form the Women's Research Center of Boston. The group included Carol Brown, who had just gotten her sociology degree from Columbia and was working with David Gil, a Heller faculty member; Liz Fox, who had her psychology doctorate from Harvard; Roz Feldberg, a newly minted Ph.D. sociologist from the University of Chicago; Jan Cohen, another recent Ph.D. sociologist and also a single mom; Joan Rothschild, who had a journalism degree from NYU, and Jackie Ballou a young social worker who dropped out of the group after a short time. Our first project was to learn about the Massachusetts government and how women in power might make a difference. Our monograph "Who Rules Massachusetts Women?" was self-published and sold in the local bookstores.

Next, we got a small grant from the Russell Sage Foundation to research women-headed families. My interest started when I walked with my son and his friend Albert one afternoon. I overheard them talking about a third boy in a lot of trouble. The other boy said, "Well, you know his mother is divorced." I thought, "Wait a minute, I'm divorced, and my son isn't in trouble. Aren't there kids in trouble who are living with two parents?"

So, our group began an exploratory study in which we identified and interviewed thirty divorced women raising children. We selected a sample representing white, Black, and Latina women, both poor and middle class. We were looking not from a pathology lens but from a strengths perspective. How were they managing? What problems did they face? What were the structural impediments in their lives? For several years, we met weekly, writing and rewriting drafts of chapters. Have you ever had a committee try to write a book? We could never complete it, but we did write several published journal articles and gave talks at conferences. I was even interviewed on the local Paul Benzaquin TV show.

These, we argued, were not "broken" families, which was the common parlance to describe single-parent families. This was personal for me. The problems kids sometimes displayed had been created by the turbulent household before the divorce. Recently divorced families were often troubled, but those who had been divorced longer had reached a new equilibrium. This idea came from my class with Cal Takagi. We realized that divorce is not just an event but an evolving process. Most had lowered living standards, but as one mother told us, "He was just another mouth to feed."

Another mother with three teenage daughters lived in a housing project. She said she wanted to work but had to stay on welfare because the project was a dangerous place, and she needed to be home to supervise them so they wouldn't get into trouble. We, like many feminist sociologists, were discovering exploratory research and treating those we questioned as human beings rather than "subjects" with important stories to tell. I learned so much from my companions, attending *Sociologists for Women in Society* conferences with them and being exposed to political economy theories espoused by Carol and Jan. All this while I was supposed to be working on my dissertation—I should have changed my topic and used this research. However, I came to Heller to work with Prof. Warren, a community sociologist. I didn't think he was interested in family or feminist issues.

The Newton schools had an excellent music program. Lorena started playing the cello, and I would take her for her weekly private lessons. Garth, now in first grade, signed up for Little League, and I would grade papers sitting in the stands while watching their three-hour, four-inning games. These six-year-old boys (girls were not yet allowed to play) rarely hit a ball, and Garth, in the outfield, often watched a bird or picked a flower instead of paying attention to the game. Eventually, he would become a skilled athlete.

When Lorena was in fourth grade, there was a fall festival at the Williams Elementary School playground. She went early, and when I got there with Garth, she was leaning against the fence, holding a tiny ball of black fur in her hands. It was a little kitten. Some smart parent had figured this was a good place to get rid of her cat's litter. "Mom," she begged, "can we PLEASE keep her?" How could I say no? The kitten was crazy, jumping around, trying to catch butterflies, and running all over the house, so we named her *Mashugina* (Yiddish for crazy). She was Lorena's cat, sleeping on her bed until she went away to college, at which point Mashugina deigned to sleep on my bed.

My $400 monthly stipend wasn't going far. I couldn't afford any clothes and certainly couldn't go out. Those first four months were tough—adjusting to Boston, to a doctoral program, getting the kids adjusted, and having no money. I had tried to get a loan, but I couldn't get a student loan because I wasn't dependent on my parents and had no other resources. I was running out of the $1000 I had saved. I was ready to quit.

Ted had come for a visit and urged me to see the dean and tell him my plight. When I did, tearfully, Dean Gurin was very kind and understanding. "We want you to learn about welfare; we don't want you to live like you're on it." In my sense of fairness, I didn't think I should get more than any other student. We all received the same $400/month, but some were veterans with benefits, some had wives supporting them, and some had consulting jobs or trust funds. Arnie Gurin arranged for me to be a teaching assistant in the class he and Marty Rein were co-teaching that spring.

When I entered the school, I hadn't wanted to tie myself down to a particular area of human services such as child welfare, aging, or developmental disabilities. That's where the federal funding for fellowships came from. Because I was interested in community organizing, the school gave me a fellowship from a private foundation instead. The problem was that with the change of deans, no one had bothered to seek funding for my second year. Again, I would be in financial trouble. Marty Rein, who was now at MIT, knew Frank Baker at the Harvard Laboratory of Community Psychiatry. He was starting a research project exploring social change in the Boston United Fund and Planning Council.

I was hired as a Research Associate. If you know the Boston culture, being at Harvard is like being at God's right hand. They all take themselves very seriously and believe their own hype. I won't bore you with my job, mainly as a "non-participant observer" sitting in on meetings, taking notes, and analyzing what took place, using systems theory. I learned a lot about systems theory, which I have used in many contexts. My officemate, a British sociologist Ruby Abrahams, thought we were making "good money for a woman." I earned what I had in Seattle three years previously, before finishing my master's degree. I was not satisfied with what was considered a good salary for a woman!

Having left Seattle to attend Brandeis in Massachusetts, I thought that was the end of the relationship with Ted, but after a year of loneliness, I was open to his suggestion to move in with me. This was the situation: I had a piano he used for composing. I paid the rent and bought the food. He paid for his daily bottle of wine and for his laundry to be done. He argued that I had been paying for everything else anyway. Every night, we had wine with dinner. I would have one glass, and he would finish the bottle before the end of the evening. If there were an open bottle of wine, Scotch, or any other alcohol, he'd drink until it was empty.

How was I so stupid that I didn't demand he make more of a contribution? Mel had almost never supported me, so it didn't occur to me to ask him to help support us. I was lonely, and managing with two small children was hard. He was supportive emotionally, and I needed someone to talk to. Finally, a few things happened that made me end the relationship. First, I invited a fellow student and his wife over, and Ted, who had probably been drinking, got into a terrible argument with Dave about artists, hollering and cursing. He was very defensive about how artists should not be held to the same standard as ordinary people. I think this was a Nietzschean argument, and it bothered me. His out-of-control behavior mortified me.

The last straw was how he related to the kids. Garth, now six or seven, had had a tough time with the move, was gaining weight, and occasionally reverted to bedwetting. With his Germanic background, Ted would not tolerate this and decided to spank him whenever he wet the bed. I knew that was the wrong way to handle it, and I did not want him hurting my child, emotionally or physically. I told him to move out, and he moved back to Seattle.

The Heller curriculum underwent changes the year before I came because of the radical class preceding me. They threw out preliminary exams and replaced them with a substantive paper, which they never defined. I wrote one the length of a dissertation—I thought it had to be substantive! I finished my coursework in one year, as they had eliminated most of the requirements. I took a non-credit colloquium with Professor Gil. Each week, we discussed one chapter in John Rawls' new volume, *"A Theory of Justice."* Both other faculty and students from different years sat in, and all participated as equals. It was one of the most stimulating courses I ever had, and I made a lifelong friend with another student, John Else.

I was working on my dissertation proposal. I had chosen Roland Warren as my chair, but in my second year, he was on sabbatical. Dave Austin, an assistant professor on my committee, praised it, but when Warren returned, he rejected it without giving me any guidance. I revered the man, a tall, sixty-year-old, distinguished, patrician-looking pacifist, a brilliant writer, and a stimulating teacher. But one-to-one, I could not get him to engage. He was not helpful, and I didn't even know what questions to ask. I think he was disappointed that I didn't choose to work on the topic he was interested in, and he had no interest in my subject. I wanted to understand social change, but seeing that as overwhelming, I chose to look at organizational change within the United Funds and Councils, as my job was collecting research in such an organization in Boston.

I worked, spent time on our single-parent research project, and was raising the kids. I usually had a boyfriend during this time but didn't have him come to the house. Lorena was getting older, and I had heard stories about men and young girls. Also, my life was complicated enough. It was a good recreational release for me, but at this point in my life, I did not want the complications of a committed long-term relationship.

When Ted was still living with me, he had introduced me to a friend from high school who had just moved to Boston. Leonard was a violist and had had relationships with both men and women. He was a high-strung (pun intended) strawberry blond, very bright, and a compulsive eater and smoker who had just lost about eighty pounds on Weight Watchers. After Ted and I broke up and he left town, Leonard called me and asked me to help paint his new apartment in downtown Boston.

After a few hours of painting, he suggested driving to Maine for a lobster dinner. I had never been to Maine and had never eaten lobster. That was the start of a short sexual relationship but a long friendship. One night, after making love in his apartment, he announced he had to leave, obviously to pick up a man. That was it! In the early 70s, I didn't understand much about being gay and thought he could turn it off. When I realized he was sleeping with others, I ended the relationship, but I did urge him to come out and attend the new Gay Rights Parade in Boston.

Over time, we resumed a non-sexual friendship. He saw my kids grow up and always brought them gifts from his trips with boyfriends. We could talk, and I learned a lot about gay life from him. Over time, he could not control his weight, became extremely obese, developed diabetes and dementia, and finally entered a nursing home. I would call him every year on his birthday, and then, three years ago, I called and learned he had died.

Several years ago, during Presidents' Weekend, I took the kids to the Boston University retreat center in New Hampshire, where we learned to cross-country ski. We'd stay in a bunkhouse with a stove, ski all morning, come back for lunch, ski all afternoon, have dinner, and then play some ping pong before falling sound asleep. We did this for several years, renting and waxing the skis.

In the fall, we would take a Columbus Day weekend trip to Cape Cod. I'd pick up a bucket of Kentucky Fried Chicken, and we'd sit on the big bed in our motel room watching color TV! The following days, we'd swim in the motel pool, take long walks on the beach, and get some fish and chips for dinner.

At home, we'd have family day on the weekend, and they could pick where to go. It was either bowling or a movie because I couldn't get them into a museum after a certain age! Every night was talk time. I'd sit beside each of their beds, and they would talk about their feelings or what had happened that day. No wonder I had trouble finding the time and focus to work on my dissertation. I needed help.

The school had a ten-year deadline, and I was completing my fifth year. Then, an unexpected encounter motivated me. Wyatt Jones was a sweet, kind faculty member known to help weaker students struggling to complete their dissertations even, it was rumored, to partially write them. I was at the local Safeway, and after exchanging pleasantries, he said, "I understand you're having trouble completing your dissertation. Would you like me to become your chairman?" That was a jolt! I would not be one of those students! I would retain Warren as my chair, as unhelpful as he had been. I was now mobilized to complete my proposal, which was finally accepted.

I sent the kids to Seattle to stay with my parents while I worked on it that summer. This was a win-win-win situation. I wanted my kids to have a positive father figure and role model. Between my father and Jay, my brother-in-law, this would be great for them. It was also suitable for my parents, who missed having their grandchildren nearby. They got to spend time with them. And it was good for me to have a respite from caregiving and focus on myself for once.

In 1975, I again sent my kids to Seattle with my parents for the summer so I could go to Europe for a month. I had never traveled abroad. When other young people were hitchhiking around Europe in the '60s, I was already married with kids. I bought a student Eurail pass that gave me unlimited train travel on the continent and planned my itinerary to visit London, Paris, Vienna, Venice, Florence, and Nice, with a return to London. I had my Frommer's guide *Europe on $5 a Day* and would try to keep to that budget.

I was excited but fearful. In the journal I kept at the time, "A Journey to Europe and Into Myself," I expressed both my anticipation and fears before leaving and then impressions during the trip. Several of the quotes sprinkled through this narrative are from that journal. The night before going, I wrote:

"…it really hit me as I was reading about Venice. I suddenly began sobbing, clenching my hands together. Finally, I will be getting to see all the sights, sounds, and smells I've read and heard about all my life: the Brontes' novels, *Tale of Two Cities, Death in Venice*…the train ship to Paris and the White Cliffs of Dover…*The Merchant of Venice*, Michelangelo, Van Gogh, Notre Dame. These are all part of my memory bank, and now, to finally see them."

Then, the next morning, my fear took over: fear of being killed, fear that I'd lose myself while traveling, fear that something would happen just before I left and that I would never go. I tried to keep recounting a friend's story of a woman approached by a man on an isolated beach. Instead of being raped or murdered, they started a friendly conversation, he was an American pilot, and she got a ride back with him on his plane. Again, my fear of men, fear of their becoming violent if I expressed myself too strongly. This trip would be an exploration into myself and an opportunity for growth.

I traveled by myself for four weeks. I did have some friends to visit in London and Paris, but for the first time in my adult life, I was alone, with only myself to account for. I did make all the tourist stops but also had many serendipitous adventures. I got picked up by a few men before I learned to avoid all eye contact. I began my journal, which kept me company while eating alone in cafes. I didn't have to look at couples or wonder if they were looking at me, a woman alone. I just wrote and wrote—about my feelings as well as my experiences. I've continued this practice, especially when traveling. When I returned after a month, I felt stronger and more confident in my ability to manage. I realized I enjoyed the challenge of new cultures and languages and learning to find my way around a new city. I felt refreshed and reinvigorated.

In the summer of 1976, I settled down to work on the big D. Now that the proposal had been accepted, it was just a matter of following the outline, a road map, completing the research, and writing the damn thing. As a faculty member at Boston University, I could commandeer a small carrel, a little room just big enough for a desk and chair on the fourth floor with a long, narrow window overlooking the Charles River floating peacefully below. I could see the rowing team and the sailboats and wished I was down there, with the calm water and blue sky.

Each morning, I'd get to the library no later than 10:00 a.m. and work until it closed at 10:00 p.m. I took breaks for a quick lunch and dinner on Commonwealth Avenue, where the library was located, and sometimes took a break and stalked the stacks. That's when I started reading books about Emma Goldman, Rosa Luxemburg, and other fiery women radicals as a break from the dissertation. By the end of the summer, I had completed the first draft. The kids were back, and I had a full teaching load at the School of Social Work. I would work on polishing it to graduate in June 1977.

Then, an unforeseen accident befell me; I fell. Like most winters in Boston, that winter was very snowy, and the streets were not cleared of ice. Garth, my friend Elk, and I were walking in Cambridge, enjoying the first sunny day in March. The streets were crowded, and I, in my usual impatience, didn't want to tarry, so I walked around the edge of the curb. I didn't see the black ice and took a terrible fall. It was evident that I had dislocated my shoulder. I've had two children without medication, but this was the most excruciating pain I had ever endured. Fortunately, Elk had his car there and rushed me to the hospital. During the car ride, I remember biting my lip as tears ran down my cheeks, not wanting to cry out as I didn't want to scare Garth. At the hospital, I was administered morphine for the pain. The doctors then set my dislocated shoulder and put my arm in a shoulder sling that I would need to wear for six weeks to keep my shoulder stable as it heals. It was my right arm, so that I wouldn't be doing any writing, and then my muscles atrophied to the point that I couldn't even lift my arm. Six more weeks of physical therapy! There went plans for completing the dissertation by June!

That spring of 1977, Garth was about to turn thirteen and was getting ready for his Bar Mitzvah. When he was younger, he did not like Sunday School, so I didn't insist he continue, but now he wanted a Bar Mitzvah. I suspect it was because some of his classmates had them and he saw the presents they received. I arranged for a tutor, a college student of Al Axelrad, the charismatic reform rabbi of Brandeis Hillel. One day, Garth said, "Wouldn't it be nice if my father could come to my Bar Mitzvah?" It was as though a knife had pierced my heart. All these years, we had no contact with Mel, but at one point, Garth asked for a photo of his father, which I supplied to him. Garth kept it near his bed.

What should I do? I consulted both with Marty Rein and Danny Stein, Mel's two uncles, who were both social workers. They both strongly recommended that I not invite him. "This is Garth's Day. You don't know what he might do, and that memory will last. Tell him when he is eighteen, if he still wants to see his dad, you'll help him find him." A few months passed when I sat Garth down, explained why I didn't want his father to come, and showed him that crazy letter he'd sent before the divorce. I think I was taking it more seriously than he, as he seemed pretty blasé about the whole thing.

Garth's Bar Mitzvah

The ceremony was held at the Brandeis chapel, a small, intimate setting where Rabbi Axelrad presided, and Garth performed admirably. I was able to use the Heller lounge for the reception. I had arranged for a caterer. Garth asked for and got a chocolate cheesecake for dessert. I invited all the family from Brooklyn, and my parents came out from Seattle to help. It was a joyous occasion. After the Heller reception, many of the family returned to my house, where I put on tapes of Yiddish and Israeli songs. Some of us danced, and later, we ate the leftovers from the reception.

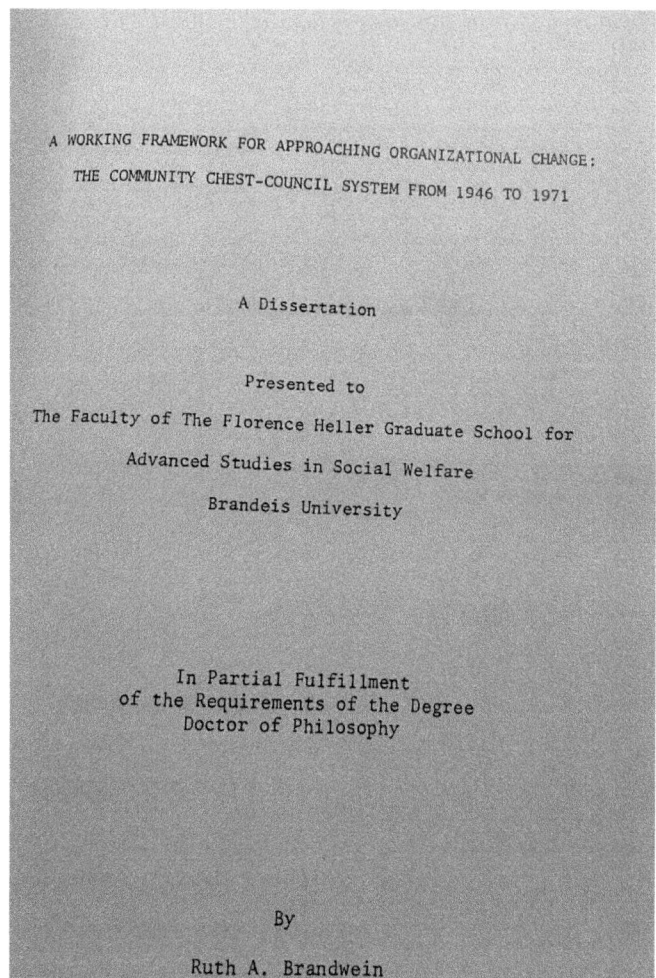

A WORKING FRAMEWORK FOR APPROACHING ORGANIZATIONAL CHANGE:
THE COMMUNITY CHEST-COUNCIL SYSTEM FROM 1946 TO 1971

A Dissertation

Presented to

The Faculty of The Florence Heller Graduate School for

Advanced Studies in Social Welfare

Brandeis University

In Partial Fulfillment
of the Requirements of the Degree
Doctor of Philosophy

By

Ruth A. Brandwein

Cover page of my Doctoral dissertation – 1977

Finally, with the kids in Seattle for one more summer, I completed the dissertation and passed my orals in the fall of 1977. The school had no December graduation, so my Ph.D. was officially conferred in June 1978. Before that, I had been approached by several social work deans for junior positions, but when they learned I had not yet completed the dissertation, they were loath to hire me. They had too many experiences of junior faculty coming as ABD (all-but-dissertation), getting involved in resettling in a new location, preparing new courses, and never finishing.

By now, I was in my fifth year as an assistant professor at Boston University School of Social Work. I was initially hired in 1973 for one year, teaching social policy under Professor Louis Lowy, a brilliant teacher, a real *mensch,* and another mentor. I needed a job to support my kids. I almost took a job at a new social work school in Eau Claire, Wisconsin. Fortunately for me, the plans for the school fell apart, and so did the job. After first being hired on a one-year contract, the school then rehired me as a full-time, tenure-track assistant professor to head up the Planning, Administration and Community Organization concentration. I loved the school, the other faculty, and the students.

I was given free rein to develop new field placements in innovative settings such as ACORN (a radical organization that no longer exists); 1199 SEIU, a progressive union; settlement houses; the new State Office for Children; and the Department of Human Services. I had obtained funding there for placement of a student unit with top administration and a paid field instructor. One day, I got a call from one of the administrators. She complained that one of my young male graduate students was coming to their office with a scruffy beard and torn jeans. I called him into my office and told him about the complaint. A young radical, he claimed, "Well, that's who I am."

I said, "Are your values so superficial that they come off with your jeans?"

I agreed he could keep his beard, but it had to be neat, but no jeans.

This was a professional office. He complied. Years later, I learned he was the director of a U.S. Department of Health and Human Services regional office. I hope he kept his radical principles!

At the time, Boston University's president was John Silber, who many believed was a truly horrible man! The first thing he did after being hired in the late 1960s was to invite the police on campus to quell a student uprising. By custom, campuses were sanctuaries from police interference, but not only did they appear, they bashed heads. He also relentlessly punished radical faculty like Fran Piven and Howard

Zinn. They were tenured so that he couldn't fire them, but he made sure they never got a raise in all the years he was president. After three years and many faculty complaints, his board, which he had stacked with some of his old buddies from Texas Instrument Company, sent out what was to be a confidential evaluation questionnaire. Some of us who were untenured knew better than to complete it. Sure enough, one of the senior faculty, Lennie, who was active on the Faculty Council and very critical of Silber, was honest in his assessment and taken to task—I guess it wasn't confidential after all!

Faculties, especially at private universities, do not identify as working-class members and are usually hostile to unions. It had reached such a point, with Silber channeling surpluses to an endowment account and then claiming there was no money for any faculty raises, that the faculty decided they really did need a union to protect themselves. The president hired union busters and did everything possible to prevent the union. Eventually, the courts determined that as faculty, they were part of the administration because they made decisions on curriculum and faculty hires, so they were deemed ineligible to have a union. Silber later ran for Governor on the Democratic ticket, and all my friends voted for his Republican opponent because Silber was supporting Bush's Iran-Contra efforts, and they feared his using it as a stepping stone to run for President.

Lenny used to stop by my office in the school and kid around. He was smart and a lot of fun. One evening, we were at an event when he suggested, "Let's go to bed." I demurred, and he asked, "Why not?" I couldn't think of a good reason, so we did and began an affair that lasted about a year. I'd go to his apartment once a week. I didn't have time for anything else between the kids, working, trying to write my dissertation, and my weekly meetings for women's research. As a social worker, he would want to talk about our relationship, but I would brush him off, wanting just to enjoy it. He thought I reminded him of my father. I said he was wrong. He was a lot older than me, Jewish, and from Brooklyn. But he was nothing like my father in looks, temperament, or politics.

He had a summer house on a lake in New Hampshire, so after taking the kids to Seattle, where they would spend the summer, I returned after a few weeks and met him in Montreal for the World's Fair there. The plan was to drive to his house afterward, where I would stay for a few weeks working on the dissertation, away from distractions. On our way back, we were stopped at the Canadian border. He was suntanned, wearing sunglasses, and driving a convertible with a younger woman beside him. I guess we were profiled because they asked us to open the trunk to inspect our luggage. When they opened mine they found a small plastic bag with green herbs. Very suspicious! Lenny's first remark was, "I don't know anything about that." I explained that I had come to Montreal from Seattle, where I had purchased this bag of herbs for cooking at the Pike Place Market. I didn't even remember the name of the herb. That sounded like a fishy story, so they told us to wait outside and took the bag inside for analysis. I was angry at Lenny for his immediate reaction to protect himself. I feared I could be framed because inside, they could switch the bag with some marijuana they might have previously confiscated from some other traveler. After a few intense minutes, they reemerged and sent us on our way, but he had pushed the button of my distrust of men.

Nevertheless, we had a good time that summer, watching shooting stars in August from his deck, swimming, reading, working, and making love. But by the fall, he seemed restless and finally admitted he was starting to see someone else but couldn't make any decision. I decided that instead of retreating, I would fight to keep him. This continued until New Year's Eve, when he waited for me to decide for him so he wouldn't feel guilty about the breakup. He complained about shoulder pains that he was getting from his terrible dilemma. Finally, I decided I had enough and did him the favor of ending it.

After the relationship ended, I felt sad, depressed, and upset, although the relationship had not lasted long. It seemed my reaction was out of proportion to the breakup. Perhaps I was reliving the breakup with Mel. That finally prompted me to start therapy for the second time in my life. I had done so when I first got to Seattle, with a social worker at the mental health clinic, who helped me work through some issues so I wouldn't make the same mistake I had made in getting involved with Mel. Now, Carol Brown recommended her therapist, but when I went to see her, she felt I had worked out my issues with women but now needed a male therapist. She recommended her husband, Dave Nichols, a psychologist, who I continued to see until I left the Boston area. After addressing the Lenny issue, he helped me realize that part of my block against completing the dissertation was that I was afraid of surpassing Dad, who had always been the "smart one" in the family. Would I lose his love if I became a Doctor? Dave gave me a reality check: "You've already surpassed him in education and accomplishments." When we terminated counseling, I had completed the dissertation and was headed for an excellent new position in Iowa, and he sent me with his blessings by predicting, "I think you're now ready for a good relationship."

In my fifth year at Boston University, I would have to come up for a tenure decision the next year. The policy was up or out. Silber was not awarding tenure to anyone in any of the social sciences. My friend Roz Feldberg, a brilliant, published sociologist, had been turned down for tenure. I was sure I didn't have a chance and could be out of work at the end of next year. My friend from Dave Gil's seminar, John Else, was back in the Midwest, teaching at the University of Iowa. He urged me to be interviewed for the school's director position. Every spring, the Council of Social Work Education held a conference that, besides boring papers in small, stuffy rooms, was a meat market for faculty hires. Search committees would interview prospective hires, huddling in the restaurant, in the lobby, in their deans' suites, or wherever there were a few comfortable seats. That year, the conference would be held in New Orleans. I had a paper accepted so the school would pay my way, and I could be interviewed there. I was excited by the prospect of giving a professional paper and finally visiting New Orleans.

That year was the deadline for ERA passage by state legislatures. Not surprisingly, Louisiana did not pass it, so the women's movement was boycotting the state. Reluctantly, I called the Iowa folks to tell them I would not be attending and why. (It would be another forty years until I finally got to New Orleans!) I didn't realize that their faculty was so progressive that this decision was a factor in my favor, and they invited me to visit the University for a three-day interview process.

At the old, huge Chicago O'Hare Airport, I had to transfer to a smaller plane. Finally, my plane arrived at the Cedar Rapids airport, where I had to descend the plane stairs and walk across the tarmac to a small, one-story building. Meeting me was John, along with some colleagues, all looking to me, the sophisticated Easterner, like a bunch of hicks. Neither their hair nor their clothing were stylish, but I soon realized these were warm, smart, caring people. The school emphasized social development and a strengths, rather than a pathology perspective. It seemed like a perfect fit, and I loved the place! This was the kind of school where I would be comfortable sharing their values. I guess they loved me too because they offered me the position of Director of the School.

So now I had to decide what to do. I had to discuss this with my kids. Garth was in junior high school, and Lorena would be entering her final year of high school. I never did know quite what was going on with her issues with other kids, but she was eager to leave her school. So here were my choices: Stay in the Boston area and be out of a job in a year, or move to Iowa City for double my salary, promotion to associate professor with tenure, and director of the School of Social Work. I decided after about ten days. Boston acquaintances could not comprehend how I could leave Boston, the Athens of America, and the center of the universe.

CHAPTER 7

On the Move Again—Iowa

Once again, we were on the move. They say you have to move out if you want to move up. That's what professional men have always done to make a better living for their families. I'm the head of my family, and this was a very good professional move. We found a three-bedroom house with a finished basement with a bedroom and bath so Garth could have some privacy from the women. It had a big yard and was only about six minutes from the university. The retired former director of the school lived down the street, and another faculty member, Jeannie Williams, was right across the street.

The school's director reports to Howard Laster, the Dean of Arts and Sciences. May Brodbeck, an eminent philosopher, and an older single woman, served as Vice President, while Sandy Boyd, an open and pleasant individual from the Midwest, was the President. I liked them all, and they were very pleased to bring in an outsider with my credentials. The school was small and not distinguished, so their strategy was "grow your own." Very fitting for a farm state! Instead of trying to hire a senior, established person, who they probably could not attract (or afford), they took a gamble on me, believing in my potential.

Iowa was a real culture shock. "Everyone is blond and bland." Yes, mostly blond, Scandinavian, or other North European extraction, and if not bland, then pleasant, and friendly, but it didn't seem to go any deeper. As the newbie with a title, everyone was very welcoming. I was invited to parties and got to know people in other departments. I especially liked Linda Kerber, a brilliant feminist historian whose husband taught in the medical school and played with a chamber music group. I was sometimes invited to the Kerbers' when his quartet was playing. Linda and I had many stimulating conversations about women in social welfare history.

The first thing I did was to hire four new faculty, two recent Berkeley graduates with newly minted doctorates. Several of the local faculty had only their master's degrees. I was trying to make the school more academically legitimate within the university. Schools of social work often have low status in a research university because we are more hands-on and practice-oriented.

We had three satellite campuses: one in the Quad-Cities, less than an hour east, near the Mississippi; one in Des Moines, the capitol, a good hour straight west on I-90; and another in Sioux City, about a six-hour drive, in the northwest corner of the state. There was one on-site faculty in each place, but the rest of the faculty alternated their schedules and often carpooled to the sites. I realized that all that car travel had a positive unintended consequence. Faculty got to know each other informally and chatted while driving so that by the time a decision had to be made at a faculty meeting, the issues had already been thrashed out.

The campus was situated in downtown Iowa City with a thriving women's bookshop, coffee house, and an authentic college town ambiance. Farmland began on the outskirts of town. Roads were straight, at right angles along the perimeters of farm tracts. It took about two days to find my way around, unlike the meandering, diagonal, wiggling roads in the east. Iowa weather was not my favorite part of living there. Spring was muddy. All that rich black soil practically oozed up from tractor trenches. The summers were hot and humid, and if you stepped out of the air-conditioned house in the evening, it was so humid you thought you were stepping into a Turkish bath. The fall, well, fell. We had a little tree in front of the house that still had leaves in the fall. I was away for the weekend, and the leaves were all on the ground when I returned. The maples, oaks, and other hardwood trees you find on the east coast weren't here. But I did begin to appreciate the subtle, pastel-like color changes of the different grasses contrasting with the emerald green of soybean leaves in the gently rolling hills along the highway.

The winter was treacherous. Iowa is right on the cusp between the snow belt up north in Minnesota and the rain to our south in Kansas. So, what did we get? Ice storms! I was the last one out of the building on the day before winter break. I always like to work late when everyone is gone and the office is quiet. When I got to my car, the lock was frozen. Finally, with some help, I could open it, only to glide into a van on the other side of the road as I was trying to make the right turn, curving up the hill to our house. Fortunately, there was minor damage, and being Iowa, the friendly driver told us to forget it. We both just wanted to get to our warm and dry homes. Another day, I was supposed to drive out to Des Moines after a night of a snow and ice storm. As I made my way very slowly on I-90, I passed several overturned-trailer trucks on the sides of the road. I could go only about fifteen miles an hour, which would have gotten me there in about a week. I turned around and went home!

I wanted to visit our Sioux City campus, so a faculty member who was due to teach there and I chartered a small four-seater, single-engine plane at the nearby airport. I got in next to the pilot, and the faculty member sat in the back seat. Once we were aloft, the pilot turned to me and asked, "Do you want to fly it?" There were two sets of instruments. I guess the plane was sometimes used for lessons. "Sure!" So, for the next forty-five minutes, I was flying the plane! It's easy; besides moving the steering wheel left and right, you move it up and down. It was a perfectly clear, cloudless day, and I could look down at the houses, farms, and occasional hedgerows of trees. It looked like a green and brown checkerboard. Once again, as I had fourteen years before on the flight to Seattle, I felt a sense of freedom as I soared above the earth. And this time, I was really in control. But, like the 9/11 pilots, I had not learned how to land it. To my relief, our pilot took over as we got close to Sioux City.

One of my first challenges occurred just about a week after I started. Dean Laster called me into his office and told me that a male student, placed in a state legislator's office, had complained about an edict published in our weekly school newsletter. John Else and I had worked on a gender-neutral language policy that all students and faculty were asked to use. The student had shown it, complaining to this conservative state legislator who, in turn, had complained to our university president, telling him in no uncertain terms that only the Legislature sets policy. I was flabbergasted and outraged. "If this is what being an administrator means then I don't want the job!" In his soothing manner, Dean Laster replied, "Just give me an academic rationale for this. We have autonomy on academic issues." I returned to my office, cooled off, and thought through the issue. I had good reasons to offer. First, a social work code of ethics calls for respect for all individuals and promotes social justice. Second, I quoted from the guidebooks of some academic publishers now requiring non-sexist language. I wrote this up, gave it to the dean, and that was the end of that little dust-up. I learned that instead of getting angry, I needed to use rationality to justify decisions that were challenged.

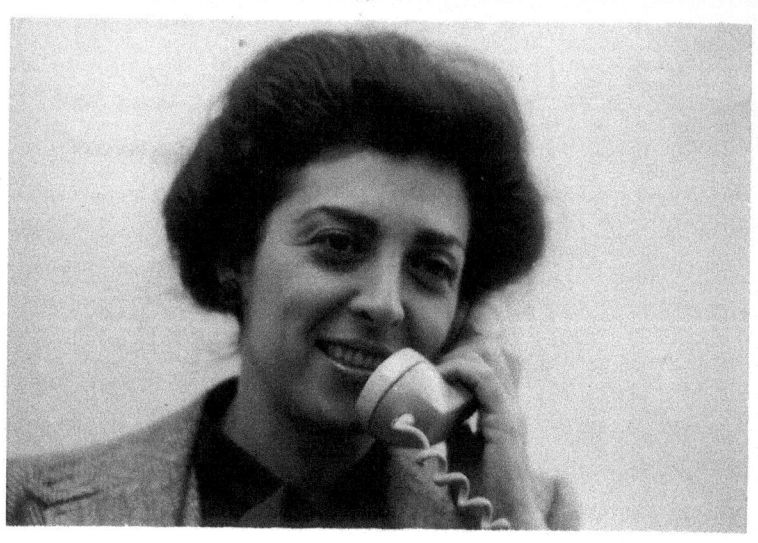

In my office at the University of Iowa School of Social Work

The kids seemed to be adjusting well. Lorena landed the part of Juliet in the senior play soon after we had arrived. We had a ping pong table down in the basement, and Garth and I used to play fiercely competitive games. Garth was now in junior high and was not doing well. He couldn't seem to master French and had a group of friends who were a bit wild. Once, they got into trouble for trying to break into parking meters just for the hell of it.

This was farm country, so kids could get their learner's permits at fourteen so they could drive the family tractor. Lorena wasn't interested in driving, but Garth got his permit just after he turned fourteen. I was doing a lot of traveling back then. The kids were old enough, I thought, to be left alone as there were neighbors nearby if needed. One night, when I got home late, I found a piece of paper on the kitchen table. It was a traffic citation. I woke Garth up. "What's this?" He was only allowed to drive with an adult in the car, but he had taken out my blue Dodge Dart with a friend. They were speeding down a street and didn't realize it was a cul-de-sac and ended up bouncing over the curb and stalling out on a neighbor's lawn.

I was furious! He wasn't charged with speeding because the officer hadn't actually clocked him while driving, but the skid marks and the chewed-up lawn were noticeable. I read him the riot act. "If you were a Black kid in the city, you'd be sitting in jail now, but because you're white, we live in a nice area, and your mom is a big shot, you got away easy." I was also mad as hell because he had broken the axle in the car, and the repairs would have been excessive. I reduced his allowance for months to help pay for the repair, but I finally bought another car.

The following year, Lorena graduated and started Grinnell. It was an hour away. She had applied to Harvard and other schools but accepted when Grinnell offered her early admission and scholarship aid. She had decided she liked the idea of a small school in a little town with low brick buildings and lush green lawns. When I dropped her off at her dorm and saw her walking inside, I sat in the car and began to cry. How dumb was I! I thought my job was done once my kid was in college. I had raised her independently for the better part of her eighteen years. I had no idea that being a parent never ends, and sometimes, the most challenging times are when they are in college and even after graduation. And I didn't realize I'd feel like an empty nester when she left home.

As a boy living in a home with two females, Garth had separated and individuated much earlier. He was interested in sports, and while we loved each other, we didn't have much in common. Lorena and I had been very close, maybe too close, so it really left a big hole when she left. A surprising result was that Garth and I got closer after she was gone.

The first Thanksgiving that Lorena was in college was memorable. Because our home was close, she brought about five kids home for the weekend; students whose homes were too far and too expensive for a trip for just the Thanksgiving weekend. They put their sleeping bags all over the living room, and the following day, everyone joined me in our big country kitchen to make the turkey with stuffing and trimmings and about five quiches for the vegetarians.

I wanted to take advantage of everything there was to learn about living in the Midwest. Everything was new, different, and another adventure. We went to the state fair in Des Moines, where I saw a life-size cow sculpted in butter by a woman sitting in a refrigerated room behind a glass wall. I thought, "This woman could have been a Michelangelo; her work is superb, but instead, she is a farmwife in Iowa sculpting cows." We also went to the Threshers Fair, where we saw old farm instruments that had been used over the years. We visited the nearby Amana colonies, settled by Amish or Mennonite families in the 1800s. They had made the Amana appliances before being sold to a larger company. I never did get used to the old Amish men with Oshkosh overalls and suspenders,slowly driving their buggies down the highway.

Mom and Dad came out to visit, and we drove up to northern Iowa to Spillville, where Dvorak had stayed when writing The New World Symphony. We also saw a clock museum with everything from small, wooden carved cuckoo clocks to enormous grandfather clocks that chimed in deep tones. We stopped for lunch at a little restaurant, and while seated, a woman came up and very shyly asked me, "Excuse me, but, but are you, Anne Bancroft?" In those days, with my large brown eyes and dark hair in a high bun on top of my head, people often said I resembled her. Before I could say no, Mom countered in a hushed voice, "Please, we don't want any publicity!" The poor woman smiled knowingly and tiptoed away. To this day, she is probably telling everyone about the day she met Anne Bancroft.

"Mom," I cried, between giggles after the lady was gone, "How could you?"

"I didn't lie. I didn't say you were Anne Bancroft."

This became one of our family stories, and we continued to get a laugh over it whenever we recounted it. Mom did have a wicked sense of humor that persisted, even years later, when she had Alzheimer's.

Every seven years, schools of social work must be reaccredited by the Council of Social Work Education (CSWE), the national accrediting body. This would be my first major challenge for our masters and undergraduate programs, which I had not anticipated. Fortunately, my friend John Else took charge of the reaccreditation process and did a terrific job leading it.

We involved all the faculty in different facets of the report and finally chose our visiting team. They met with the faculty, university administration, students, and agencies where students had their field placements. It all went very well, but one of our visitors was shocked when she asked about junior and senior faculty, and everyone looked bewildered. Unlike most academic programs, the school made little distinction between the different ranks, leading this visitor to remark, "This is like a Marxist commune." We had the closest thing to a classless society!

Iowa City was a pleasant college town, but I knew I didn't want to spend the rest of my life there. Some faculty from other departments had talked about the golden noose of tenure—once you have it, you get stuck. Unless you're a superstar, no other university will hire you with tenure, and most of us value the security of tenure too much to give it up. One woman faculty who was not a native, remarked, "You know you've been in Iowa City too long when the turquoise pantsuit in the department store window starts to look good."

Bob, a Love Story

In the fall of 1978, I attended my first deans' meeting in Washington, DC. I met another new dean who had just started at Bryn Mawr. He was tall, slender, and mild-mannered, with blue eyes, reddish-blonde hair, and a beard. He looked like a young god! As we chatted, I realized I had met him at the Heller School years before. He had also worked with Roland Warren and had been two years ahead of me. Once, while meeting with Warren, he asked me if I could give Bob a ride. Of course, I would. So, Bob folded his long legs into my tiny VW Beetle, and I dropped him off at his home in Newton. When we recounted that first meeting, he recalled, "Boy, was your car full of trash." I hadn't made a good impression on him then.

The next deans' meeting was in Boston the following February. We had agreed to get together there. That evening, after the meetings concluded, we went out for dinner. As I recall, the place had disco dancing. I had never done that, but he was such a beautiful dancer that I felt carried away by the music and his gentle but firm leading. I've often remarked that I'll only let a man lead me when I'm dancing!

That week, we had numerous long conversations touching on various aspects of our lives—our children, our new jobs, and our political views. We talked at length, catching up on each other's lives. I learned that he, like my father, was a pacifist and had been active in the civil rights movement. He had even spent a year at a historic Black college in the South as a white minority student. He and his former wife had been Peace Corps volunteers in Nicaragua. We were clearly entranced with each other. It was a magical week. Dave Nichols, my therapist in Boston, had told me when I was terminating counseling that he thought I was ready for a healthy, mature relationship. Now I felt ready.

A month later, we met at a halfway point in Covington, Kentucky, where we spent the weekend. That's when he told me he had had a homosexual lover when he was married. He said his wife had not minded, which had even helped their relationship. I had only known one homosexual man previously, my friend Leonard, in Boston. Leonard was gay and very open about it. Bob did not believe he was gay or even bisexual. I asked him whether he preferred men or women. Without hesitation, he said, "women." I took him at his word. In the '70s, many young people had been experimenting with their sexuality, which is how I perceived it. It sounded like this was an experiment and was in the past. I knew nothing about bisexuality then. I was naïve and thought nothing more about it until much later. I invited Bob to visit me in Iowa City. He did, and he met the kids. Lorena immediately took to him, Garth less so. Garth was more the jock type, which Bob was not. By now, Bob and I had fallen in love.

In July 1979, the kids were in Seattle, so Bob and I spent three weeks together, first in Bryn Mawr and then at a place he rented on

Long Beach Island. It was a seaside town in New Jersey that he knew and loved. A few strange things that should have sent up red flags happened then. One evening in Philadelphia, we had gone to a club called "The Black Banana." I'm not sure if it was a gay cub because it was dark and noisy, but I think there were some gay couples there, too. Bob seemed to know the place. After a short while, he insisted we leave. He seemed upset. For about an hour outside the club, he kept talking. I don't remember the conversation, only my feeling of anxiety. Everything had seemed so wonderful between us; what was going on? Then, one day at the beach, I noticed him looking at some slim young guys in bikinis running around. That night, he reacted strangely, distancing me. These little disquieting moments were buried in my happiness.

It was on that vacation that he first proposed marriage. Finally, as I was reaching forty, I would have an entire life with a partner I could be proud of. It was over twenty years since my marriage to Mel, who was so different. I believed Bob was so wonderful, so perfect—the man of my dreams. He was good-looking and brilliant, and his values were like mine. We were in the same field. He did not feel threatened by my intellect but encouraged and appreciated my ideas. He was a feminist. I knew our peers and other professors respected him, which meant a lot to me. I felt I had met my equal. I knew my father would like him for his pacifism and liberal ideals. It was perfect, or so I thought.

In late October, I visited him at his home on the idyllic Bryn Mawr campus, where I met his youngest son, Tony, who was living with him. Tony was about ten at the time. He had two older sons, Peter, the oldest, and Kevin, just a year younger. We played tennis, although I didn't know how; I met his colleagues and was very happy. The next deans meeting was in San Antonio in November. We disco-danced again and walked along what was then the new Riverwalk in the evening. We were enchanted by the lights from the restaurants along the bank reflected on the water. After the conference, we drove down to Tijuana, Mexico, a terrible, dirty city with pigs eating garbage in the street where half-naked prostitutes strolled. We slept in an awful motel, bought a piñata, and had lots of fun together. For the winter holidays in 1980, Garth, Lorena, and I joined Bob, Tony, Kevin, and Peter at Bob's big home on the Bryn Mawr campus. He had a large, decorated Christmas tree. We exchanged gifts and had a New Year's Eve party with all the kids. We had a great time! It seemed we were one big traditional family.

In February, he and I attended another deans' meeting, this time in Los Angeles. Afterward, we drove south to San Diego to meet Bob's elderly father, Sidney, a retired Methodist minister. During this trip, I felt some qualms about the relationship sustaining itself. But he talked again about us getting married. I did not feel the need for a legal marriage; I didn't relish the role of "wife," but I was not opposed to it if he wanted it. We began to think about where we could both get jobs. There didn't seem to be anything available at Bryn Mawr. Now that I think about it, there were so many other schools in the Philadelphia area, but I never pursued that. I tried to find a place for him at the University of Iowa, but they had a strict nepotism policy.

In April, I got a call from Steve, who had been in that radical class at Heller the year before me. He was now teaching at a new school of social work out on Long Island, and they needed a dean. Would I be interested? He emphasized that it was a school of social welfare, not social work. The first dean retiring was Sandy Kravitz, another member of that same Heller Class. Steve explained that this was a school with a mission of social justice, policy, and change. I had never anticipated moving back to NY, and certainly not Long Island. In my bohemian college days, Long Island was the epitome of middle-class, square, bourgeois life I had avoided like the plague. Still, maybe there was a chance Bob could find something in the New York area.

I got a call from a woman who was Vi Seider's niece. Vi had told me all about Joan, another community organizer, social worker, and social justice advocate. Joan Ohlson had briefly been on the Stony Brook faculty. She warned me against going to Stony Brook. She said it was a "snake pit" with warring factions and a toxic atmosphere.

I was invited to Stony Brook for an interview. The school facility, the faculty, and the administration turned me off. The vice president, Howard Oaks, was a dentist. His assistant, who was very enthusiastic about my coming, seemed somehow untrustworthy. The Health Sciences building housing the school was a high concrete edifice, towering over the beaches, farmlands, and small suburban communities of one-story homes. It looked like a monstrosity, so out of place, towering over the still pastoral North Shore of eastern Long Island. In addition to the social welfare school, this lumbering giant housed the hospital, Medical School, Nursing School, and School of Health Management. I was informed it had more square feet of space than the Empire State Building!

What I did like about the school was its mission statement emphasizing social justice and working with vulnerable populations. And I fell in love with the students. Many were returning older women and minorities. So different from lily-white Iowa!

As I was mulling this over, Bob got an offer from Fordham University School of Social Work in New York City for a full professorship. Here was our chance to be together. As for the warning about Stony Brook, I reasoned that I had had a positive time as director (same job, different title as dean) in Iowa. Being a feminist, I utilized a management style that emphasized collaboration and inclusion. In my hubris, I believed I could handle the New York situation. Besides, this was a chance for us to be together. So, we decided to take both positions.

Because our reaccreditation process at the Iowa school would not finally be approved until the fall, I did not believe it would be ethical for me to leave to start my new position in the fall of 1980, so I postponed my start to the beginning of the second semester, starting in January 1981. Bob would not be starting at Fordham until the fall of 1981. That summer, we were going to travel together to Seattle to be married, but when he got to my house before the start of our trip, he said, "I don't think I want a formal marriage." I think he was concerned about his financial obligation to his three children. I was a little taken aback, but as I never really wanted the role of "wife," we decided to have a ring ceremony at my parents' home. After all, my parents had also lived together for years before formally marrying.

We traveled I-90, camping one night at the Wind River Refuge in the Rocky Mountains of Wyoming. The narrow road wound around the mountain, hugging the cliff on one side and a sheer drop-off on the passenger side. Bob was driving. I was paralyzed with fear while absorbing the beauty of the landscape, trying to focus on the blue, snowcapped mountains in the distance. We arrived at the campsite, a taking-off point for serious hikers continuing up the mountain. A large meadow was strewn with brilliantly colored wildflowers, a stream with a large boulder to one side, and mosquitoes as large as hummingbirds. They were ferocious. They were voracious. I don't think they had smelled human blood for days. We had to huddle near the fire, and I appreciated Bob's cigar smoke for the first time. That helped a little before we quickly crawled into our pup tent and hid our flesh under our sleeping bags.

My parents were delighted to meet Bob! They were so happy I finally found a good, smart, sane man with their values. I think they had always been worried about my not having remarried. In their world, a woman was not complete unless she had a man, and not just a man but a "good husband." After all my crazy earlier rebelliousness, I was finally turning into a good daughter. My children, sister, and parents were all at the dining room table when Bob and I exchanged vows of commitment and placed wedding rings on each other's fingers. For all intents and purposes, we felt married. Then I returned to Iowa with the kids, and he met up with Kevin and went down to San Diego to visit his father.

One touching Iowa memory is of Bill's bar mitzvah. It was a bar mitzvah like no other. Bill was a developmentally delayed man in his sixties. During the deinstitutionalization movement of the 1960s, he was released from an institution for the "retarded," where he had dwelled since childhood. His father had died, and his mother had trouble caring for her several children, so he and his siblings were sent to an orphanage. A few years later, when the orphanage was closed, he was sent to a "School for Retarded Children."

Who knows what his mental capacity was or could have been, but living all those years with others with developmental delays and no intellectual stimulation, he exhibited the same behaviors, except that he loved to play the harmonica—especially polkas! Upon his release, he was "adopted" by a young man named Barry, who moved to Iowa City to teach at the School of Social Work and took Bill with him. Bill was put in charge of the school's coffee room, where he could dispense coffee and make change, with some help. It was also a way to help students see someone with disabilities as a person, not a client.

Bill loved religion. He'd go to church weekly with his landlady, who had rented him a room. Somehow it was learned that he was Jewish. The one rabbi in town took him under his wing. Bill wanted to be bar mitzvahed, but there was no way he could learn the prayers, much less read from the *haftarah* (an ancient Hebrew text). Instead, his prayer was playing the harmonica. There wasn't a dry eye in the synagogue.

Despite the general laid-back tolerance in Iowa, one ugly incident reflected insidious antisemitism. I was on a search committee for the state Director of Social Services and recommended a Brandeis colleague. Martin was by far the most qualified candidate, having held a high-level position in the New York City Welfare Department and helped the State of Israel reorganize their social services department. He was invited for an interview, and I thought he handled himself exceptionally well. Yet, when the committee met again to review the finalists, his name was not on the list. I asked the Governor's assistant why, and she replied, "He wouldn't fit in." When I pressed her, she replied that his shoes weren't shined. Then she finally added that "He may be right for New York but not for Iowa, where he would have to get his budget passed by the Legislature." When she said New York,

I heard "Jewish," and the hairs on my back fairly bristled. Perhaps he wouldn't have "fitted in." She obviously didn't know I was also Jewish and originally from New York.

The last few months in Iowa were sad and sweet. We did get a glowing reaccreditation report, and the faculty gave me a warm and joyful going-away party with some fun gifts. I kept two for many years—a large metal corncob. My short sojourn in Iowa is memorable. I would be in for a rude shock back in New York.

PART III
STONY BROOK AND LONG ISLAND

CHAPTER 8

Aggravation, Love, And Death

Garth was upset about the move to Long Island, as he was in his first year of high school and didn't want to start in the middle of the year. I arranged with a faculty member, John Haynes, and his wife, Gretchen, for Garth to live with them in the fall and start school at Northport High School, where they lived. It was a good school district, only about a half hour from Stony Brook, and that's where I thought we would find a home. It was only about an hour's train ride into Manhattan, where Bob would work. This turned out to be a good experience for Garth. Living away from me, he had to learn how to do his laundry, become more independent, and be on his best behavior! John and Gretchen were lovely people, and it worked out well.

When Bob and I came out to look for a house, I thought, "There's no 'there' there." Miles and miles of suburban one-family homes of various sizes, with the obligatory patch of green lawns marked off by wide avenues lined with strip malls and car dealerships. I recently found something I had written then entitled "Alienation: Thy Name is Long Island or What's a Nice Academic Like You Doing in a Place Like This?" In it, I compared Boston and Iowa City, both university towns quite different in size, to Long Island. I had moved from Boston, the "Athens of America," to Iowa City, the "Athens of the Midwest."

Long Island was no Athens. Instead, it was the epitome of the consumer culture. I bemoaned no public transportation, no public indoor pool, fewer women's organizations, and few bookstores; no one answered the NOW phone, and the women's health clinic, unlike the one in Iowa City, did not perform abortions.

Furthermore, services were scattered through numerous villages or commercial centers. I wrote in my journal, "I have found that there is no center, no heart, no focus to the sprawling, suburban metropolis known as Long Island. There is no sense of place, no sense of belonging, no identity…."

Bob said, "If I have to live in Long Island, I want to live on the water." We finally found a recently built three-bedroom home in Centerport on the north shore of the town of Huntington. It was on Centershore Road, a dead-end street with Centerport Harbor across the road. This was the second from the last house on the street before the road ended on a path to Centerport Beach.

My home in Centerport, NY

The house, set on a double lot, had no basement, as the land was too close to the water level. It was a modern, cedar-paneled home with long rectangular windows facing the harbor. It had a one-and-a-half car garage (not for half a car, but for extra storage.) The inside garage door opened into a utility room, a half bath, and the kitchen.

The kitchen window in the rear of the house faced a steep hill, so we had no neighbors behind us, and to the right of the garage, a steep staircase led to a home on the street at the very top of the hill. A sliding door at the far end of the kitchen led to a brick patio with a grape trellis and a large lawn.

The front door, up on a rise from the street, opened onto an atrium hallway with a spiral staircase ascending to the second floor. On the ceiling above the atrium and staircase was a skylight (that later proved to be just a pane of glass that leaked water, created mold, and eventually had to be replaced.) The architect who built the house had creative ideas but used cheap materials. There were two areas on either side of the hallway. One became the dining room, the other the library and music room. It was an open floor plan, so the only walls were to the kitchen downstairs and the bedrooms upstairs.

One of my first purchases was a used baby grand piano. Upstairs, open from the atrium, was a large living room, split in two by the spiral staircase. The living space to the left of the stairs had a free-standing stove and a set of sliding doors leading to a wooden deck that extended to the main bedroom. The living area to the right was smaller, had a built-in bar, and could hold a couch and one chair. There were two additional bedrooms and a full bath. Another staircase led to a double attic that was wired for electricity. This would serve as a dorm when Bob's sons visited.

By now, Lorena was in her second year at Grinnell College in Iowa, so only Garth would be living with us. Tony was back in North Carolina, living with his mother, Kevin was in college, and Peter was working and living by himself in North Carolina.

I put the house in Iowa City on the market, but it had not yet sold by the time we left in December. I had to get a bridge loan for half of the Centerport house. Bob and I had purchased it as owners in common with the right of tenancy in the entirety (that means if either of us should die, the other had a right to remain in the house even though the other's heirs would own half.)

Lorena and I loaded up the car and drove across to New York. On the way, we stopped off in Columbus, Ohio, to visit my childhood friend Goldie, who was living there with her husband, Hank. We couldn't take our cat, Mashugina, with us, so we had a neighbor feed her and was to ship her by air two days later when we would have arrived in Centerport. Unexpectedly, the weather turned bitterly cold, and the airlines refused to send animals because they would have frozen in the baggage compartments. It took two weeks until she arrived, and by then, she was severely traumatized by having been alone in a house all that time and then flying in a baggage carrier.

That was not the only fly in the ointment. It was Christmas week, and Bob wanted a tree, which I had no objections to, but I would not abide having a manger with baby Jesus and angels in my home. He was not happy about that. We also argued over little things: whose pictures to put up or whose blender we should use. He insisted on removing the wallpaper upstairs and replacing it with seagrass paper. He wanted things his way. I was not as insistent or thought these were not worth fighting over, so in most cases, except for the manger, I let him have his way.

He was also rigid about finances. He wanted us to keep our finances separate, and instead of just splitting the house costs, he divided them proportionately based on whose kids were living there at different times. So, when Lorena was home for the beginning of the month, I paid three quarters and Bob one; when Tony was there for a visit, it was 2:3; when Lorena left, it was 2:1. Why did I give in to that? I don't know. It seemed fair as I would be earning more as a dean than he would as a faculty member, and I didn't want to fight over finances. Was I reverting to the old behavior of not asserting myself when living with a man?

He seemed uneasy around Lorena, a nubile teenager who could be overly demonstrative. He also thought I was spoiling Garth. When his kids were around, I thought he was too uninvolved. They would leave the house, and he would not even inquire where they were going or when they would return. Our childrearing styles were utterly different.

Then there was Stony Brook. Among the faculty were several tenured men, most of whom had been there at the school's inception. Robert and Steve had been Heller School classmates of Sandy, my predecessor as dean, and both were "armchair Marxists." They saw the faculty as the "workers" and me as the capitalistic "boss." Robert had been acting dean the semester before I arrived. I asked him why he hadn't been named dean. He said he hadn't wanted it. I learned that their first choice for dean had been Eunice, another classmate of theirs. I had also been friendly with her at Heller. When she was interviewed, the vice president rejected her. I asked Robert to be the associate dean, but he refused, so I chose an untenured Puerto Rican faculty member. Angel got along with everyone and was a very detail-oriented manager. Just what I needed. So, I arranged for Angel to have the large office across from mine. This was the associate dean's office. Robert had occupied it, but he had turned down the associate position.

One day, Robert casually sauntered in (that's how he usually entered a room) and said, "Oh, I guess I will be your associate dean" (like he was doing me a favor). I said, "I'm sorry, but I've already offered it to Angel." Bob had known Robert at the Heller School and had no respect for him. He thought he was sneaky and a hustler. I'm sure his opinion influenced my perception of him.

I met individually with each faculty member to get to know them. Three young women without PhDs were acolytes of Robert or Steve. I didn't know if there was anything else in their relationships, but they were all very chummy. The men protected them, and in turn, they supported whatever positions those male faculty took. I suggested that the women might want to pursue their doctorate. As I had at Iowa, I was trying to strengthen the school's academic credentials. At the time, many of the faculty were in non-tenure-track positions and without doctorates. Without any job security, they were at the mercy of the tenured faculty, who periodically had to vote on their reappointment.

I learned that the school had been conceived as a twelve-month program, much like the other professional schools in the Health

Sciences Center, where our school was located. However, the School of Social Welfare had opted for a ten-month program, like other social work schools. When Howard Oaks took over as Vice President and saw no one was around during the summer, he reduced faculty salaries to ten months but allowed the school to retain some of those extra funds for "summer salaries." The four original male faculty members were getting "summer salaries" but not working during summer. That did not seem fair to me. Instead, I thought the female, non-tenure-track field faculty, who did work during the summer preparing the field placements for the fall, should get reimbursed. I also introduced the Council of International Programs, which we had in Iowa, to Stony Brook and asked another professor to lead it. I paid her a summer salary as well.

Boy, had I asked for trouble! It might have been fair and rational, but taking away an extra summer salary and a big office did not endear me to the tenured male faculty! Angel often cautioned me, "Ruth, you're being too rational." By the end of my first semester, things were heading to a boiling point. I suggested we have an all-day retreat. We had done that annually in Iowa, and it worked wonderfully. There, we met in a different venue, talking informally about issues, with breaks for lunch, volleyball games, and relaxation.

I scheduled our retreat at the university's Sunwood Retreat, a mansion on the water in the posh Belle Mead neighborhood. The vice president had turned down my request for an outside facilitator. One or two of the male faculty made presentations about finances that made it appear that I was being dishonest. No one except one or two junior faculty would even speak to me. It was a horrible experience! My stomach was in knots, and I was ready to quit! I decided that leaving a job after only five months would look bad for me professionally, so I was determined to stick it out for at least two years.

Bob had been commuting from Philadelphia on the weekends as his dean position at Bryn Mawr went through the end of the spring semester. One weekend in the summer, as I was relaxing on our lawn after breakfast and Bob was smoking his ubiquitous cigar, we saw a car approaching down our street. "I wonder who that could be?" said Bob. As the car pulled up and six buff young men emerged, Bob said, "Oh, I invited my men's group from Bryn Mawr, but I thought it was next week."

He hadn't told me anything about this. These men were part of a student men's group he had started and led because the school was predominately women, and he wanted men to feel more comfortable at the school. I thought it odd that he would be in that relationship with students. He was much chummier with these students than I thought appropriate in a dean's role, but maybe I was just uptight.

I tried to be gracious, welcoming them, and prepared the dorm in the attic for them as they were staying for the weekend. Bob suggested that I might want to go off and do something with friends or go shopping at the mall. No! This is my weekend, my home, and I have been looking forward to a quiet weekend to recover from the tensions I faced all week at the school. So, by turns, Bob took them out on the Sunfish we had purchased while I tried to relax and went for a swim. We had dinner together, and at the end of the evening, in my pent-up fury from the entire day, I suggested he might want to go upstairs and sleep with the men. Of course, he said he wanted to sleep with me, and he did.

We did have some good times going up to Lake Nineveh in Vermont, where he had purchased land in a Quaker community. We'd go up for a week, camping, swimming, canoeing, picking blueberries, and cooking over the campfire that Bob, a Boy Scout, was an expert at preparing. Other times, when he seemed to be in a funk, I would suggest we take a trip or do something. He answered, "Things would seem nice on a trip, but it doesn't solve anything." I didn't know what it was supposed to solve.

We had a comfortable routine at home that summer. Bob was the most disciplined person I knew. After breakfast, he'd go upstairs to his office and work on his next book, with maybe a short lunch break until 4 or 4:30 pm. Then, he'd have his cigar and a drink on the patio. It got me into a more disciplined routine. I was working on a paper on sexism in community organizing. He supported my ideas, asked perceptive questions, and made helpful suggestions. It was a real partnership of two academics. When it was published, it made a real contribution to the profession.

We visited North Carolina the following spring to see his sons in Asheville. We made a bet on how far south we would go before we started seeing flowering trees. Whoever won the bet would decide where we would go for ice cream upon our return. I won the bet and wanted to go to Baskin and Robbins, up the hill from us on Washington Drive, for their unique ice cream with M&M bits. He had wanted to go to the shop in Northport Village that made their own ice cream, but I insisted on going where I wanted as I had won. He pouted about that, took his ice cream, and went to sit in the car to eat it. I was so angry that I decided to walk home. I had no idea how long the walk would be at night on a curvy road with no sidewalk. He didn't try to follow me in the car to pick me up. He never apologized when I finally got home.

Another time I felt he was entirely uncaring was the day we went to Ellwood, the next village over. We drove down Ellwood Road, and I had to stop at Monroe Music to pick up some music for Lorena, who was still playing her cello. Bob would proceed to the intersection of Ellwood and Jericho Turnpike to a large hardware store to pick up some needed items. The plan was that I'd walk down and meet him there. I had not realized how far a walk it would be. It was probably two miles down to Jericho Turnpike. I kept looking at cars going in the other direction, hoping he had finished his errand and was coming back to pick me up, but no.

I finally arrived at the store, and Bob wasn't there. This was before cell phones. I wasn't sure what to do but used the store phone and called the house. Bob answered. When I didn't arrive at the store, he just left! I called a cab and finally got home. This "perfect" man was turning out to be not so perfect, but that was before the actual problem surfaced.

In 1983, my parents were celebrating their 50th wedding anniversary. Gale and I decided to have a big party at my home and invite all our East Coast relatives. We had it outdoors in June, with an extensive buffet table under the grape arbor. We had a caterer who prepared cold, dilled salmon. Tante Ida, Cousin Nettie, Bob and Lisa, their infant, Aunt Lil and Uncle Herb, and many others came. The lawn was filled, and everyone had a great time. Gale and my parents stayed for a few days afterward before they left on their anniversary cruise.

At my parents' anniversary celebration, shortly before Bob's death

Bob had not been feeling well; he was tired and seemed flushed. We attributed it to all the company and excitement. After they all left, we decided that getting to Vermont for a few days would be good. We always had a relaxing time there. The next morning, we climbed the hill to pick wild blueberries for pancakes. Bob was still feeling tired and seemed to be running a low-grade fever. But we got along well, and I remember our making love out in the open, leaning against a large rock. That was the last time.

When we returned, I insisted he see Dr. Calderbank, his internist. Because Bob had had a fever like this some years before, and because he and his wife had lived in Central America, the doctor was sure it was some bug that Bob had contracted, the effects of which he would overcome, as he had in the past. However, he did a skin test and found his immune system did not respond, so he sent us to Dr. Nash, an infectious disease specialist looking into an emerging disease. He thought Bob had AIDS! AIDS? We were both in denial. In 1983, very little was known of this disease, and less about the causes. Bob thought it was only contracted by gays who were doing drugs. He decided he did not like Dr. Nash and didn't want to go back.

By the fall, his fever spiked, sometimes to 103 at night and then going down to near normal in the morning. At first, it could be controlled by aspirin. He had been losing weight and started having night sweats. Then, it was September, and school had started. I'd leave for school in the morning, returning in late afternoon, and make him a shake with eggs and bananas—anything to fatten him up! He was staying in bed, so I'd sit at the edge and we'd play backgammon. I had access to the best doctors there in the Health Sciences Center at Stony Brook. I consulted Dr. Fritz, a very kind, smart man who chaired the Internal Medicine Department. He came to our home, examined Bob, and confirmed that it was probably some blood-borne infection he had contracted in the tropics, and he would eventually recover. We were both very relieved to hear that.

But he didn't recover. He got worse. Aspirin was no longer controlling his fever. The night sweats got so bad that I had to change the sheets and put towels under his burning body. We finally realized that he might have AIDS. Then he revealed that while in New York City, he occasionally went to the baths (where gay men would meet for sex). First, he said two or four times. At a later time, he said it was six or eight times. I remembered all those evenings he had come home late.

I recalled how once he had asked me how I would feel if he had another companion. I was clear. I would not tolerate another lover. He said no more. I had thought we were having a hypothetical conversation, and I made my feelings clear. I would not allow the same kind of situation I allowed with Mel. I had no idea he was looking for a male lover. I had such ambivalence. I felt very loving and didn't want him to die and tried to be supportive, but I was angry that he had been deceptive. Another man I had trusted! Because he did not want to lose me, he did not admit what he was doing, thus depriving me of making my own choice.

I spoke to his brother Ron, an out-of-the-closet gay man in San Francisco with a long-term partner. I had visited them a few times when Lorena was living there after having graduated from Grinnell. I told him I was angry that he had introduced Bob to the baths. He replied that it was better than Bob had previously been doing— hooking up with men in public restrooms.

His breathing was starting to sound labored. Because we had rejected Dr. Nash, we were referred to Doctor Kaplan at Long Island Jewish Hospital in nearby Nassau County. Finally, one night, I feared Bob would stop breathing and die in our bed. I took him to the hospital emergency room. Dr. Kaplan, a youngish, pleasant man with tremendous knowledge of this new disease, was there to meet us. He took an X-ray of Bob's lungs and was shaken to learn that his lungs were 30% filled with water. When he left for a few minutes to get some other equipment, Bob asked me to read what had been written in his chart. "Mr. M, a fifty-two-year-old white bisexual male..." I read aloud. Bob cried out, "I'm not bisexual." Even then, he was in denial about his identity. He was admitted to Intensive Care, where he remained for five weeks until he died on November 3, 1983.

Those five weeks were a nightmare. During the day, I was dealing with all the crap at Stony Brook. Then I would leave early and drive an hour and a half in rush hour to the hospital, where I'd see Bob getting weaker every day. I would talk to the doctors. I'd go home to the local school where I took a dance aerobics course a few days a week. I've often imagined that the high heartbeat and sweating burnt the AIDS virus from my body. At night, I'd sometimes read a book of bad Polish jokes to laugh myself to sleep, a la Norman Cousins, whose book said laughter is the best medicine.

After a few weeks, Bob's sister Marge and his son Peter came out, and Kevin returned from Paris, where he had been studying art. We'd take turns at Bob's bedside. One day, Marge and her partner, Jean Audrey, insisted on taking me out shopping. Like Bob's brother Ron, Marge was gay, but both accepted their sexuality. One day, when he knew he was dying, Bob said he wanted to marry me. I thought about it—that way, I would inherit the house. But I didn't know what his medical insurance would cover, and I feared that as his widow, I'd be left with a massive mountain of medical debts after he died. Besides, he hadn't wanted to marry me before, so I said no. Marge witnessed him signing his will. She and I started planning for his cremation and memorial service.

In addition to pneumocystis pneumonia in his lungs, he developed cytomegalic virus, an opportunist infection. They had put him on prednisone, which was very new then, but Dr. Kaplan said the cytomegalic virus was the killer—they had nothing to fight it. We all have these viruses in our system, but healthy bodies easily fight them off. Bob had thrush in his mouth, and his feet were caked with what looked like a mossy fungus. His body was being attacked, and he had no immune system to fight anything off. He was barely conscious.

It was now late October, and the ride to the hospital was painfully beautiful. The sky was blue, and the changing trees seemed more brilliant in reds and golds than I had ever seen or perhaps had never noticed. Life was going on while Bob was dying. I believed that he would die the day the trees started shedding their leaves. I was wrong.

The trees were still ablaze on November 3 when he died. Marge, the boys, and I were all there. I was in the room when the machines he was plugged into started going flat. We had previously told the doctor we would not have him code blue to restart his heart. There was no point in putting him through that.

They had never questioned whether I was his wife, although we had different names. As a heterosexual couple, there was never a question about my right to determine the course of his treatment. How different it would have been if we were a same-sex couple. I watched the machines go flat and called in the doctors. They asked me to leave the room, determined that he was dead, and cleaned his body. Then they said I could re-enter.

Then, the strangest thing happened. His body, once racked with infections, now looked healthy again. Blood flowed back into his extremities, and he appeared fit and beautiful once more, as I had known him when we first met. I removed the covers to take one final look and bid farewell to his long, lean, tanned body. We had lived together for just under three years.

CHAPTER 9

Living Without Bob

For three years after Bob's death, I was consumed by fear that I had contracted AIDS. Whenever I had a sore throat, a slight fever, or a cough, I wondered if that was the beginning…but then I'd be okay. A year or two later, a test was developed for HIV, but I was afraid to take it. I feared that *knowing* would be my death sentence. After a while, I realized that the fear was eating me up, and I had read—it turned out it was erroneous information—that not everyone who tested positive would get AIDS or die. So, I finally convinced myself to take the test, as I could no longer live with the uncertainty.

During all this time, there was so much stigma about AIDS that I didn't tell people how Bob had died. I had confided in my vice president and asked his advice about sharing it with the faculty. He advised against it. Even my parents did not know. I had told them it was some tropical fever, which Bob's doctors had initially thought. Dad had such respect for Bob, and Mom was so pleased that I had finally had a relationship with the "right" man; I didn't want to shatter their illusions and break their hearts. In retrospect, I wonder if they did know or at least suspect, but we never talked about it after his death.

One of my good friends, Cecile, lived on Long Island. I had known her since high school and asked her to accompany me for the test at a Nassau County facility. I was somewhat well known in health circles in Suffolk County and feared people finding out. There were two tests—the enzyme-linked immunosorbent assay, Elisa, and the Western Blot.

I had both tests, as the Western Blot had a relatively high error rate. I had to wait two weeks for the results. These were the longest, anxiety-filled weeks of my life. When they both returned negative, I cried, sank down on my lawn, and kissed the earth, thankful for my life. This experience has made me understand the fragility of life and the importance of living it to the fullest, as we never know when our future can suddenly be shattered.

I had been advised not to make any significant changes in my life after such a life-altering event. So, although I wasn't happy at Stony Brook, I felt that emotionally, I did not have the strength to look for a new job and a new place to live. I dug in and said to myself, "If I can't be happy, at least I can be productive." And I was. Subsequently, I wrote several articles and book chapters, gave talks at our national social work conferences, held positions in national organizations, and started working on creating a new feminist journal.

Even before Bob died, I had been named Chair of the recently formed Women's Commission of the Council on Social Work Education (CSWE) and worked with a terrific group of feminist social work educators. One, Carol Deanow, was to become a lifelong friend.

Before Bob's passing, I became involved in another project: the launch of *Affilia: Journal of Women* and *Social Work*. Two of my good friends and senior colleagues from the CSWE Women's Caucus, Diane Bernard and Naomi Gottlieb, were published authors. However, whenever they attempted to publish work with a feminist perspective in the mainstream *Journal of Social Work*, it would invariably be rejected. This was the late '70s, and we were becoming aware of and researching sexism in social work academia. At a special National Organization of Social Workers (NASW) conference on women and social work, a few of us decided to start our own journal!

We had several obstacles on the way. We were committed to feminism in process and practice, not just in publishing feminist works. We wanted to work collectively but had to appoint an editor-in-chief. We chose Bea Saunders, who wasn't (yet) a feminist but was the only one who knew about publishing as she had been the editor of *Social Work* before retiring. We also recruited Mary Ann Quaranta, Dean of Fordham School of Social Work. We decided to include poetry and an article on practice in addition to academic articles. We were committed to providing an opportunity for young feminist scholars to publish their work and would be helpful with editorial comments to help them improve their work to make it publishable. In the first few years of developing the journal, we would meet at Bea's brownstone in Chelsea, where several of us would stay overnight. Bea's husband, a senior editor at Fortune magazine, would make and serve us breakfast! How's that for turning a seventy-plus-year-old couple into feminists? We were meeting several times a year, and that group of like-minded, bright feminist scholars became my support system both before and after Bob's death.

I joined our local Huntington NOW (National Organization for Women) chapter. When Bob and I had moved here, between the children, adjustment to the "marriage," and dealing with the tensions at the school, I had no time to seek new friends. Through Huntington NOW, I met some dedicated feminists who became lifelong friends. One, Ethel Guttenberg, recently lost her granddaughter Jamie to the Parkland massacre. Another, Abby Pariser, had difficulties with her kids, and I became a sounding board. Charlotte Koons, somewhat older, was a Wicca, and I participated in some Wiccan ceremonies at her home. Once, I brought Meg, whom I had named as one of my deputies when I worked for the County. Charlotte was reading tarot cards, and she pronounced a negative omen. Years later, I learned that Meg had been stabbing me in the back and trying to take my job. Was it a coincidence, or did Charlotte have some intuitive powers?

In 2018, at the Women's March after Trump's inauguration, I heard someone call my name. It was Charlotte, older, white-haired, confined to a wheelchair, but still a spirited feminist,.

Another involvement was unanticipated. Not very religious, I had usually confined myself to attending services only during the High Holy Days. I had done this in Boston and Iowa through Hillel on the college campuses where I worked. The one at Stony Brook was Orthodox and didn't meet my needs. I tried the Reform temple in Huntington but found it too ostentatious and not very spiritual. Eve, our field director at Stony Brook, told me about a small Reconstructionist congregation that rented a large hall and opened its doors to all for the holidays.

I liked the idea that one did not have to "pay to pray." I liked the congregation and Rabbi Arthur Schwartz, and I eventually became a member. I also liked the politics of the members. Years earlier, they had broken off from the local Reform congregation over resistance to the Vietnam War. An anti-war Catholic woman left her home to the congregation when she retired. I became a board member and chair of the social action committee. Abby was also a member, which deepened our friendship. In 1990, for my 50th birthday, I was one of eight older women who was *bat mitzvahed*, after over a year of study with our rabbi. We had all grown up in the 1950s when girls were not usually prepared for a bat mitzvah. For the first time I felt I really belonged and understood the services. My parents and children attended, although Mom had to coerce Dad to come, as he had not entered a *shul* since the death of his mother when he was fourteen. I was proud to read a small passage from the Torah that I had prepared for months. Traditionally, women were not allowed that honor.

By now, I was immersed in the feminist movement and had also become involved in international social development. I was asked to chair the CSWE International Commission and, in 1985, traveled to Nairobi to attend the U.N. Decade on Women Conference. I had not participated at the first UN Decade of Women Conference in Mexico City in 1975 but was determined to attend this one in Nairobi, Kenya. The theme of both conferences was equality, development, and peace. We were attending the Non-Governmental Organizations (NGO) conference that started a week before the formal U.N. one. Reagan was president, and his daughter, Maureen, would chair the official women's delegation. I was going with my friend Joan Rothschild, a political scientist who had been one of the members of our women's research group in Boston.

On our plane to Nairobi from JFK sat Bella Abzug, Gloria Steinem, and a large, noisy group of New York feminists. I was caught up in the excitement already. Driving from the airport after landing, we passed a huge shantytown on the outskirts of the city with its modern, gleaming hotels beyond. Our accommodations were in a three-star hotel near the University of Nairobi campus, where the conference was being held. Upon entering the campus, we had to pass through security in 1985, except for airports, which was a first for me. When we got on the grounds, I was overwhelmed by the thousands of women, many from the African continent. Some had walked for weeks to get to the conference. The Iranian revolution was only a few years old. We saw many Iranian women in their *burqas*, but some opened them to display their tight designer jeans underneath!

Tensions were high between Israeli and Palestinian women. A peace tent had been erected on the campus, where representatives from both sides took turns speaking. We were not allowed to cheer or jeer. If you liked the speaker's words, you could raise your hands and shake them, setting a peaceful, orderly tone. I don't know how much was accomplished, but it was good for us to talk and listen to one another. At another session, the first woman prime minister of Iceland remarked on the difference in the meaning of words. Men, she said, think of arms as weapons to kill people; women think of arms to hug and caress a child. Every morning, the American delegation would meet. For the first time, I learned about the different kinds of clitoridectomies and the reaction of African men to Western women interfering with their traditions. I also saw a solar cooker that would relieve women of the necessity of gathering firewood. This was an environmental issue, as this dry countryside was being denuded.

We had a break in the conference over the weekend, so Joan and I traveled to Mombasa, on the coast of the Indian Ocean. When we returned to Nairobi, we had an unpleasant shock. Delegates to the official conference had arrived, and we had been evicted from our hotel room! Ours and rooms in other hotels had been reassigned to the official U.N delegates. While we were away, our possessions had all been moved to a two-star hotel. We were lucky, though. This hotel was still in Nairobi. Some of our colleagues had been resettled in campus dorms several miles outside the city. Their complaints were unheeded. They were told, "You're in a foreign country, and the United States government can't do anything." Those U.N. delegates were Reagan appointees, and we were the "troublemakers." They couldn't prevent us from having our parallel conference, but they sure as hell weren't going to make it easy for us! Our American group met every morning to share information and experiences. We did have a liaison with Maureen Reagan's delegation, but the relationship was prickly.

When the conference concluded, Joan and I were off on our trip to Masailand with a group of about a dozen women. We connected with a women's tour group that would visit Masai women's agricultural economic development programs and a safari the week following the conference. We visited Masai Mara for a few days and saw lions, giraffes, hippos, rhinos, antelopes, gazelles, some in migration, and thousands of brilliantly colored flamingoes on Lake Nakuru.

One of the more remarkable experiences was with the women in the regional capitol in Kisumu, near Lake Victoria. Despite some difficulties, through translators, we were able to have a meaningful exchange with the women about childbearing, birth control, domestic violence, and other issues they faced. I learned that although patriarchy and partner abuse may take different forms in different cultures, they are, tragically, ubiquitous.

Portrait in Recognition League of Women Voters Huntington Outstanding Citizen Award

Upon my return, I gave slide presentations (yes, the old slide projector) to many groups. One member of the local League of Women Voters was so moved that she began a career in international development. The LWV gave me an Outstanding Citizens Award and a member painted my portrait.

The following summer, I was invited to present at two international social work conferences in Berlin and Vienna, a week apart. I arrived in Berlin a few days before the conference to visit with my former boyfriend Ted, the composer who had moved to Berlin because the German government was more supportive of serious music than the U.S. He showed me around Berlin and, contrary to my expectations, I found it to be a vibrant, diverse, and exciting city. Berlin is to Germany what New York is to the US: a more diverse population, on the edge in the arts, and more politically progressive. It is also beautiful. I had thought it would be grey and dingy, and perhaps it is during the long, dark winters. But in the summer the blossoming linden trees lined the main boulevard, where I visited the Kathe Kollwitz Museum. We also took a boat ride on the River Spree just outside the city and stopped on an island that housed an outstanding Expressionist Museum.

At the International Conference of Social Welfare, I moderated a panel on women's health. The rapporteur was a nurse from an African nation, and I was shocked at her reaction to my comments about the growing AIDS epidemic. She claimed that it was a Western disease, and they had other health issues that were of more concern. I have often wondered if she ever thought of those remarks when the AIDS plague ravished so much of the African continent!

After a week's vacation in Budapest and Dubrovnik, where I lost and later found my baggage, ate heavy Hungarian food, feasted on fresh seafood in what was then Yugoslavia, attended an outdoor concert in the old walled city of Dubrovnik and swam in the Adriatic, it was on to Vienna. This city reminded me of a matron past her prime who uses too much makeup to hide her wrinkles.

At the International Association of Schools of Social Work, I led an all-day institute on feminism in the social work curriculum. Bringing together social work educators from so many countries to discuss and share their ideas was a stimulating experience. That day and the rest of the conference went well, but the highlight of the trip on our last evening was to be the ball at the City Hall, the Rothaus. I would finally have my Viennese waltz, which I had dreamed of on my first trip to Vienna in 1975. I had brought a long dress and had persuaded a male colleague to promise to waltz with me.

The main hall of the Rothaus was high-ceilinged and about fifty feet long. We were seated at round tables with crisp white tablecloths. A lavish buffet covered one long wall. As we dined, a four-piece band wearing lederhosen played music from the many countries represented at the conference. When they played the hora, many of us, from many nations, got up and joyously danced in a large circle. Soon after was an intermission with mouthwatering desserts, to be followed by Viennese waltzes in the second part of the evening. We waited and waited, but no music. Finally, an announcer proclaimed that one of the musicians had become ill and was taken to a hospital, so there would be no more music. I was convinced that the poor man had a heart attack when he saw us dancing the hora in his Rothaus, the same place where the Austrians had welcomed Hitler.

I was staying at the home of a young colleague who had been part of our exchange program at Stony Brook. Hearing my disappointing tale, she said, "You'll get your dance." That night, we dressed up, and she took me to the Ringstrasse, the circular boulevard downtown. There were several venues playing music. She selected one where you sit at large picnic tables on a balcony on the upper level with the dance floor below.

We watched the dancing, particularly an older couple who moved very gracefully. I was getting more and more excited. At our table were two Austrian men. I kept hinting that I wanted to dance until one said, in his broad accent, "I haven't waltzed since my wedding." Okay, so he was married. I did not care; I just wanted to waltz. Suddenly, my friend jumped up from the table, rushed down the stairs, and was talking to that couple on the dance floor. Then she raced back up and told me she had told them about me and asked the woman if I could have one dance with her partner. I ran down and discovered that the couple wasn't even Viennese—they were visiting from France, but I had my Viennese waltz in Vienna with an excellent dancer. And it was the penultimate dance of the evening! Even now, I smile happily, thinking of that memory on our last night.

One benefit of sticking it out at Stony Brook was that I might be eligible for a sabbatical after six years. But I was in management, not the teachers' union that had it in their contract. The vice president, however, supported my taking a one-semester sabbatical in the fall of 1986. I felt the need to get away and considered several options.

I had loved Italy when I had traveled there in 1975, but their social work schools were more like vocational programs, and I didn't speak Italian.

Finally, Fran Piven, whom I had gotten to know when we were both at Boston University, suggested the Institute for Policy Studies (IPS) in Washington, DC. IPS had been started by Marc Raskin and Sol Landau, two radical scholars who had served in the JFK administration. They became disenchanted when the Vietnam War began to heat up, and not wanting to get back into the academic rat race, they started the Institute with the backing of wealthy liberal supporters. They published monographs and books, published a periodical entitled *New Left Notes,* and the Institute became a home for visiting scholars.

My mother's reaction was telling. When I informed my parents of my plan, Mom reacted anxiously, "But how will they manage without you?" I explained that I was leaving the school under the leadership of a troika of my associate dean and two other senior faculty. Mom responded, "What if they realize they *can* manage without you?" With mom, you couldn't win for losing. She'd always find the negative of any situation. She believed that if you thought ahead of the worst things that could happen, maybe they wouldn't, or at least you would be prepared!

I was excited to be in DC. I sublet a one-bedroom apartment on California St., off Connecticut, just a few blocks up the hill from Dupont Circle, where IPS was located. I could walk to my office. When I moved in, the office was being vacated by Bernice Johnson Reagon, the founder of the beautiful *acapella* singing group Sweet Honey in the Rock. My officemate then was a woman working in foreign policy. At that time, few women were in that field. I later learned that the institute was a sexist place. All the permanent scholars, five or six men, had sinecures. Many women, including Barbara Ehrenreich, were in and out as visiting scholars and young women were hired to do the support work, but no women were invited to be permanent resident scholars.

When I arrived, Marc had a great idea. Instead of just working alone, he suggested I develop a colloquium. I was interested in women and poverty, and with his and Fran's help, I connected with a group of brilliant feminist scholars. Among them were Heidi Hartmann, the economist who later founded the Institute for Women's Policy Studies; Diana Pearce, who developed the first methodology for determining actual income needs based on family size and structure; Pat Reuss of Women's Equity Action League, Virginia DuRivage of 9 to 5 and several academic women. We met weekly and produced a monograph entitled "Women, Families and Poverty," published by IPS. Heidi also has become a lifelong friend, and with my support, Diana became a faculty member at the University of Washington School of Social Work. I was asked to write a chapter on family policy in Raskin and Chester Hartman's (another IPS scholar) *Reclaiming America*. During that six-month stay, I also wrote an article on homelessness, but the *Journal of Social Work* rejected it because they were critical of my mixing the issues of housing and homelessness! I guess I was just ahead of my time.

I loved my time in DC. Penny White, with whom I had served on the Unitarian Universalist Service Committee board, lived just a few blocks away in the Hays-Morgan neighborhood. We'd have dinner at local Ethiopian restaurants, listen to jazz in little dives on 18th Street, walk over to Georgetown, check out historic homes, and visit the free Smithsonian museums. My favorite has always been the East Wing of the National Gallery that shows more modern works. I still remember a remarkable exhibit of Matisse in Nice. Sundays were free concerts in the West Wing rotunda. Overall, it was a very productive and enriching six months, both professionally and personally.

I returned in January 1987, and while Stony Brook was still contentious, I was getting my affirmation from the women's caucus at CSWE, *Affilia*, my publications, and my involvement in national boards and conferences. My son was now in college; my daughter had graduated and lived on the West Coast. It was just Mashugina, our crazy cat, and me alone in the house. When I had time, I would swim or kayak right in Centerport Harbor and spend some time with Florence Schiffman, a former social work student and CIP (Council of International Programs) host, who became a good friend.

In the decade of the 1980s, especially after Bob's death, I was immersed in feminism. I had helped start the successful feminist journal *Affilia: Woman and Social Work*. I was writing many academic papers and book chapters on feminist theory and its application to social work policy and practice, as well as researching sexism in this predominately women's profession.

At a Council of Social Work Education (CSWE) conference in March 1987, I met Frances Yasses, a social work educator living in India. She was impressed with my work and invited me to participate in a research project and colloquium at the Tata Institute in Bombay (now Mumbai), India. She and Vera Mehta, the dean of social work at the Tata Institute of Social Sciences, were trying to engage Indian women social work educators in feminism as well as social action. They had developed a qualitative research project pairing these social work faculty with Woman activists throughout India. They each interviewed a woman and questioned her about her work, the strategies she employed, how she had become an activist, and whether she considered herself a feminist.

Frances asked me to write an essay about my own work, using that outline. All the faculty interviewers would be at the week-long colloquium. One of the interviewees would also be present each morning and afternoon, where the educator's report would be presented and discussed. This was participatory research, so we wanted to hear from the "subjects" as well as their interlocutors.

I was thrilled with this opportunity, so after taking the necessary shots that fall, I embarked on the long air flight to Bombay. There, I was driven to the Institute campus in the suburbs, where I was given a small dormitory room with a single bed and bath. I arrived on the weekend, so after a long sleep to recover from jetlag, I did some sightseeing on Sunday.

The next morning, I was awakened by a knock on my door. A tiny Indian woman was bringing me a hot pot of the strongest, darkest Indian tea and a pitcher of boiled milk for it. I had to ask for another pot of boiled water to dilute the tea. Then I headed for breakfast in the campus cafeteria and on to our first colloquium meeting. During the week, we heard from a Muslim woman working with women in her community to assert their rights, a rural woman who had started a childcare program for poor mothers, another woman working with street prostitutes, and a Filipina woman organizing in Manila. The women I interviewed were brave, smart, and dedicated, but despite their work for women's rights, none of them identified as feminists, and nearly all lived either with their husbands or fathers. In India in the 1980s, it seemed women could not safely live independently. We social work educators bonded during that week-long colloquium, learning from each other as well from those interviewed.

I also learned how ubiquitous domestic violence is, as I had in Kenya. Although the patterns are similar, the way violence against women is expressed is different. I learned about bride burnings (*sati*), surprisingly to me, most common among the middle class, when the husband's parents felt the bride's parents had not contributed enough to the dowry. The mother-in-law would find a way to set fire to the young wife's *sari* in the kitchen. These "accidents" are known as "bride burning." I also learned of the custom of women being expected to throw themselves on the burning pyre of their dead husbands. Widows, it seemed, had no role in India. Although this practice was officially abolished, at least one occurred in a rural province during my stay.

One night, I was invited for dinner at one of the professor's homes in the suburbs. I took the local railroad train and was cautioned to travel in the women-only car. It would be unsafe for a woman to travel in those crowded cars with men. Standing in line for my ticket, I felt fortunate to be from New York, so I could shove and elbow my way onto the line with all the others, not even allowing an Indian man to cut in front of me.

After the conference, I proceeded on my own, with my preplanned tour to the Ellora and Ajanta caves, to Jaipur, Agra, and Delhi, and even a one-day trek in Nepal. With limited time and a vast country, I decided to fly between destinations. Arriving at each airport, I would hire local drivers to take me wherever I was going. They would often enjoin me to stay at their cousin's or brother-in-law's lodgings, but I always insisted on the hotel I had previously decided on, based on my trusty *Lonely Planet* guidebook. I never encountered any problems, but once, my driver stopped for a moment to pray at a small shrine on the side of the road.

No sooner had I returned from India than I got a phone call from Evelyn Roth. She was the Chief Deputy of the newly elected Suffolk County Executive, Patrick Halpin. She was starting a County Task Force on Family Violence and wanted me to chair it. I explained that I had not done direct social work with individuals or families, as my area was social policy. "That's o.k. We have many people working in organizations helping families and women, but you are well respected and won't have any agency ax to grind." What finally persuaded me to work with this visionary leader was when she told me, "I can't believe I'm now in charge of the Department of Social Services—in the 1960s, I was outside protesting for welfare rights."

The Task Force was at the forefront of approaching family violence as a systemic problem, which could be partner, child, or elder abuse. It may have been the first time in the nation to bring these three groups together. In the late 1970s, these three manifestations of violence were still in separate silos in social agencies, although social scientists were beginning to develop the concept of interpersonal violence as a similar phenomenon but with different targets for violence. We were in the vanguard of practitioners who were reframing these manifestations of violence and providing a venue for practitioners to work together. We formed committees to hold training sessions and conferences, to look at the legal and administrative systems of county government, and to support research in these areas.

Workers in the three areas were now talking to each other, working together on the committees, and discovering common patterns and problems. We brought in guest speakers, including a young man who described the family violence against gay youth. We trained bank tellers to recognize financial abuse against elderly patrons who might suddenly withdraw large sums. I was often asked to be a speaker at local conferences and interviewed on local radio and TV shows. I suddenly had an epiphany in listening to abused women and their stories. I had been an emotionally abused wife! I had never before put a name to it, nor had thousands of other women with similar experiences. The personal was undoubtedly political. I empathized with women survivors and advocated for their right to a college education. That was what had made the difference for me.

CHAPTER 10

Suffolk County Government
The Political Circus

By early 1988, the presidential election was heating up. I had an idea: I loved DC and was ready to leave Stony Brook. Maybe if the Democratic candidate won, I could get a position in the administration. Michael Dukakis was ahead in the polls in the spring. The County's Commissioner of Social Services was leaving office, and Evelyn asked me to apply for the position. I gave her a firm "no," explaining my plan to move to Washington. Well, we all know what happened. Poor Michael Dukakis was filmed in a tank wearing a helmet. He looked ridiculous. George Bush won the election. The next day, the Deputy County Executive, Evelyn, called and said, "Now, are you interested?"

A new bill had passed at the national level that would allow women on welfare to seek a college education and pay for their childcare. It seemed like an intriguing opportunity, but was I selling out? Could I really lead the Department of Social Services, which was usually cast as a villain by progressives for its treatment of women seeking financial assistance?

I decided this was a moral issue, so I sought the advice of my Rabbi, Arthur Schwartz. In his usual wise way, instead of answering directly, he advised me to read the book *Schindler's List*. This is a true story of a Polish gentile man who saved thousands of Jews during the Holocaust by putting them to work in his factories, preventing them from being sent to concentration camps.

My situation was not comparable; the Dept. of Social Services was not Nazi Germany. What I took from it, though, was that if he could work in the belly of the beast and save people during the most horrendous conditions, perhaps I could be of positive help to the Women coming into contact with the welfare department—changing the system from within. I decided to accept the position, but it would not be as easy as that.

First, I had to be interviewed in Albany by the State Commissioner of Social Services. The department was a county one but was overseen by the state, and the county commissioner position was spelled out in state legislation as a five-year term to be approved by state and county governments. Mario Cuomo was then governor, so it was a Democratic administration. The interview went well. Now I had to be approved by the Suffolk County Legislature, a group of nine Republicans and seven Democrats representing different districts in a widely diverse county with almost one and a half million residents. Suffolk County is on the eastern end of Long Island, comprising ten large towns ranging from Huntington and Babylon on the west and ending at the easternmost tips of Orient Point on the North Fork and the Hamptons on the South Fork. People think of the New York suburbs as affluent, and there certainly are wealthy enclaves. However, Suffolk is very demographically diverse: Wyandanch is a predominately poor Black community, with the Latinx enclave in Central Islip, the Shinnecock tribe in the Hamptons, and the small Poospatuck Reservation in southern Brookhaven town.

Evelyn was a consummate politician, having served in both the State and New York City governments. My first task was to meet with each legislator to introduce myself and gain their support. One day, Evelyn called me with great concern. In checking my record, it had been learned that I had been a member, and even chair for a brief time, of the Huntington chapter of NOW. What was my position on abortion? Just because abortion was legal didn't mean these conservative legislators liked the idea.

Evelyn advised that when they asked me about it, my response should be that it was a personal matter, like religion. At first, I was horrified—I wanted to stand up for what I believed in. She convinced me this was political, and I had to be pragmatic. The next obstacle was that my district legislator discovered I had donated money to his opponent in his last election. Those are public records, and he had checked who I contributed to. When I explained that the other candidate, Hope Gaines, was a personal friend of mine (and a member of NOW, but I didn't mention that), he seemed to relent. He could understand loyalty to a friend. He didn't vote for me, but at least he didn't vote against me. He abstained.

The next obstacle to my appointment was the most problematic. Unbeknown to me, Evelyn had been planning since the election of the County Executive to replace the previous Republican-appointed Commissioner of Social Services. Although it was a five-year appointment, Evelyn had been able to push her out and had planned to replace her with Rose, whom she had persuaded to move down from Albany. After some time, Evelyn had changed her mind and did not want Rose to have the position. Instead, when I arrived on the scene, she was one of the deputy commissioners while Bill, a long-time, very competent employee who was Republican, had been named interim commissioner.

Evelyn urged me not to make any firm decision for at least three months after my appointment was finalized. She cautioned that removing her would be virtually impossible if I appointed her and later regretted it. Rose and I had lunch, and I was very clear that I would not make any decision for a few months. She was pleasant but disappointed. After my appointment I did name Bill as chief deputy, as he knew the department very well, but I appointed her as another deputy commissioner.

One morning, a phone call awakened me at 3:00 a.m. A reporter called and wanted my comment on my nomination, having just been turned down by the Legislature. Of course, I responded, "No comment." Later that morning, the phone was buzzing. Maxine., a first-term legislator, had voted with the Republicans against me. Rose, an African American, had befriended Maxine, who was white and represented a district with a large African American community. Rose was angry at not having been appointed commissioner but wanted at least to be Chief Deputy, and Maxine supported her.

The vote was close, with my legislator and one other abstaining. One Democratic legislator called and begged me to hang in—we'll get it fixed, he promised. I spoke to Evelyn. She felt terrible because of her previous promises to Rose but was furious at Maxine, a fellow Democrat, who had undermined the Democratic County Executive. At this point, I was ready to bag it—in my naiveté, I had not anticipated all these political machinations. I told her that it was almost the end of the academic year, and I had responsibilities to the school. If this could not be resolved soon, I would withdraw my candidacy. It seemed I was jumping from the frying pan of the School of Social Welfare into the fire of county government.

Ultimately, Maxine changed her vote, not because of me but because of Pat Halpin, the County Executive, and her political career. Tom Downey, our congressman, was a good friend and mentor to Pat Halpin. It might hurt Pat's career if he couldn't get his appointees approved. I learned that Tom warned Maxine that her career would end if she didn't support Pat's nominee. So, I got the position, not because of my qualifications but because of political machinations that had little to do with me. My archives at the Stony Brook University library have a voluminous file of newspaper articles, editorials, and letters about this fracas.

It was as though the Progressive Era had never made it to eastern Long Island. Everything was political. I thought I had been hired because of my expertise and wanted to run the department based on what were best practices. To the county legislators, however, everything was political. Despite Civil Service, both parties tried to find ways of getting around it by hiring their own people. "Loyalty" was a big word.

From my earlier research on organizational change, I had concluded that changing the value system was one of the ways to really change an organization, so one of the first things I did was to develop a mission statement for the department. It said that we would respect the dignity of all clients. This was included in the training packet and orientation for all new employees. I visited all the offices, stopping at employees' desks and talking with them. When I went to the public assistance offices, I'd go through the public waiting room instead of the staff entrance to observe how the place looked and how clients were being treated. I considered pretending I was a client but decided against doing that, as it would have created distrust with employees.

I was determined to learn as quickly as I could about the department. I met with Bill and got a briefing, including a confidential report of his opinion on all the key administrators. I had lunch with the former commissioner, who told me she had loved the job, except for the politics of the County Legislature. I didn't quite believe her then, but she was absolutely right. I, too, loved the job. The staff was dedicated, and the organization was well-run. What I didn't love was my required appearance every two weeks before the Legislative Committee on Health and Human Services. Even the Democrats in the County Legislature were hostile to public assistance.

Soon after I arrived, there was a national recession, and more people applied for assistance. Aid to Families with Dependent Children was still a federal entitlement (later replaced by Temporary Assistance to Needy Families [TANF]), requiring us to enroll everyone eligible. The federal and state governments divided the costs evenly. However, in New York State, the state share was divided in half with the counties. That meant that when more recipients were eligible, the county budget had to accommodate them, even if that increase had not been anticipated in the budget.

A few legislators seemed to be still living in the pre-New Deal days when "welfare" was strictly a county responsibility, and they could keep people from enrolling. I heard that at one time, they had publicly listed all recipients, posting their names in front of the county building so all would know who was receiving the stigmatized "welfare." The county legislators believed that "those people" were deliberately moving to Suffolk County to receive benefits. At one point, I joked that I would stand on 14th Street in Manhattan on weekends, encouraging people to come to Suffolk to get welfare. In fact, our research showed that most people moved here for jobs or to join other family members.

When I started, several positions for department heads were vacant. A civil service test that consisted of both a written and oral examination had been administered. Prior to my assuming the position, the previous commissioner had changed the test so that instead of different ones being given for the different areas of substantive expertise: child welfare, aging, financial assistance, and others, she determined that management was generic and good managers could manage any department. The result was that a few people who knew how to take tests and were "good managers" but didn't care about our clients were on the top of the list.

One employee in particular was considered to be "to the right of Attila the Hun." When he had supervised the Medicaid program, he purposely limited approval for transportation to doctors within a five-mile radius and reduced the number of phone lines so clients could not get through to receive the required preapproval for such transportation. I was required to hire from the top three names on the list. There was a long delay between the time the test was given and when we were finally hiring. Some of the applicants had gotten other jobs by that time. A few who had scored high on the written exam failed the oral exam. But I was still left with "Attila" and others I didn't want for these key positions.

I soon learned how to play the game legally. My two deputy commissioners, one an attorney and one a political appointee of the current County Executive, hatched a plan, which I was to stay out of. They met with this employee (Attila), telling him I certainly would not choose him and urged him instead to accept a promotion to a lesser position, which he did. They did that with a few others. The result was that I was able to hire two MSW social workers to head up both Child and Adult Protective Services and another very qualified man to head public assistance. I was looking for expertise and commitment rather than politics. Two appointees happened to be Democrats, and one was a Republican. About two years later, these hires finally came to the attention of the Legislature, some of whose (Republican) members were incensed. They brought in the head of Civil Service (also Republican) to ask him about it, and he had to tell them that it had all been done perfectly legally!

One of the reasons I had finally convinced myself that I could do some good in the position was a new federal policy allowing mothers receiving public assistance to go to college and receive childcare and Medicaid while there and for one or two years afterward. From my earlier years working at the housing project in Seattle, I knew many mothers who were receiving public assistance hated it and wanted to get off but could not. I saw this as a way to help them. This was a very personal mission to me, as it was my college education that had enabled me to avoid going on welfare. I worked with the County Labor Department and the community colleges, and by the time I left, over 500 women were in college programs. Another five hundred were in non-college level vocational education, General Educational Development (GED), or English as a Second Language (ESL) programs.

I was also concerned about our child welfare programs. Some children were unable to be placed in foster care because of their severe behavioral problems and were instead relocated to out-of-state residential facilities. These were exorbitantly expensive, and we did not have the means to visit and oversee the programs. I was concerned about these kids. I could usually "sell" a program that would help clients if I could show it would save the county money. My staff developed an intensive foster care program with foster parents with prior human service training. Each would take only one or two children; we could pay them a higher rate than other foster families, but that would be much less than the cost of residential facilities. We also adopted a program that identified children at imminent risk for foster care and provided intensive case management by social workers who were on call 24/7, who visited the homes at least weekly, and had a minimum caseload.

Another successful "win-win" program was the Disabled Clients Assistance Program (DCAP). Like some of our other initiatives, it was brought to me by the staff. I was putting my feminist management style into practice. I encouraged them to come up with new ideas for helping our clients. New York State had a General Assistance program for poor single individuals not eligible for AFDC. These programs received no federal funds. Instead, the county had to pay 50% of the costs, and the state paid the balance for financial assistance and Medicaid. Many of these clients had some kind of physical or mental disability and an alcohol or drug addiction. It was a Catch-22. A person who wants to qualify for the federal Social Security Disability Insurance (SSDI) must undergo a two-step process. First, they must undergo a medical examination by a doctor. Second, they must present their case before a hearing judge. Anyone competent enough to go through those hoops and get themselves to the judge who was in another county was obviously not disabled enough to need this program.

I persuaded the county budget office to allow us to hire a few specially trained DCAP workers who would identify those General Assistance clients thought to be eligible for the federal program. Then, they would shepherd them through all the steps in the process. We had about a 95% success rate in approving them for federal disability coverage. The individuals now received higher financial payments and more security of its continuance. The county saved a lot of money because now the federal government paid half, and the county had to contribute only 25%, with the state paying the remaining 25% of their financial assistance and Medicaid coverage.

In addition to knowing I had helped the lives of many by changing the system, some opportunities arose when my decision could make a difference in one person's life. One night, I got a call from Paul, an exceptionally caring individual heading up our emergency housing program. He told me of a mother of six who had just left her abusive husband. Because the family was so large, putting them up in a motel would require several rooms at a high nightly cost. The woman was eager to return to Puerto Rico to be with her family, but it would take several days until we could get her the economy plane fare. Paul wanted to know if I would authorize emergency payment for a higher fare so they could leave immediately. In addition to the high cost of the motel, he feared that if we waited, she might be cajoled into returning to her abuser. I authorized the payment and felt good to know she and her family would be safe.

An unusual case was brought to my attention. I had an ombudsperson in my office. She answered calls for individuals and legislators and usually could address the problem, but occasionally, she would inform me of an issue. Similarly, the department heads were instructed to make me aware of situations "that could hit *Newsday*," the local daily newspaper.

One day, the head of Child Protective Services warned me that we had a case of a woman abusing her eight-year-old son with "Munchausen's Syndrome by Proxy." "What is that?" I asked. He replied that it's when a parent, usually a mother, who, in the guise of helping and protecting her child, is actually making them sick. I was incensed! It sounded to me like more mother-blaming psychobabble.

I contacted a colleague of mine at Tufts University Department of Psychiatry. She told me it was a real diagnosis; her husband had just written an article about it. Usually, it was mothers who had some background in the health field and wanted to show the medical staff how they were rescuing their children. In this case, we suspected the mother was making the child sick. He was now in the hospital, and unknown to her, we placed cameras in the room. When she wasn't present, he was improving. When she was there, he got sicker. The cameras showed that she was doing something to harm him. On that basis, we removed him from her custody.

Another case came to my attention, again making me glad I had the power to intervene. It seems a single woman was fostering an infant. The infant was healthy and white. A couple wanted to adopt, and the Foster Care caseworker was ready to remove the baby from the foster mother, who protested. I brought the caseworker involved into my office. "Was she a good foster mother? I asked.

"Oh, yes."

"Is she willing to adopt this baby she's cared for several months?"

"Oh yes."

"Then why are you considering removing the baby?"

"Well, this is a couple, and we want the child to have the best parents possible."

"Did this couple ever foster a child? "No."

"Were they willing to adopt an older child?" "No."

"What are the negative psychological consequences of removing a baby who has bonded with the foster mother and requiring her to adjust to a new mother?"

No response. As a formerly single mother who raised two beautiful, healthy children who are now successful adults, happily married, and caring parents, this was a particular sore spot for me— assuming two parents would be better for a child who had already bonded with a perfectly good mother. The idea that a couple who had never shown any interest or willingness to foster any children could now come to the agency and get a "perfect" baby galled me.

I changed the policy on the spot! In the future, the staff was required to decide on adoption based on the parent or parents' ability to be caring, nurturing, competent parents without regard to marital status. That single foster mother got to adopt her baby and confirmed my belief that one can make a difference if one lives one's values and has the knowledge to change the system.

In 1990, I was invited by the Jewish Federation Of New York to join a study group of local government officials for a weeklong trip to Israel. I had never been there and was excited by the opportunity. Our county executive and some of his staff were going, as was the county executive in Westchester; Ruth Messinger, then borough president of Manhattan; and several Jewish agency officials. Security in El Al was the tightest I'd ever seen. They didn't just ask in a routine way whether anyone had given you anything or if the luggage had ever left your hands; they looked closely and scrutinized your face and body language while interrogating you. When we finally landed in Israel, many of the passengers applauded. Before we left the tarmac, another plane arrived with Russian immigrants. Descending the plane's stairway, many of them bent and kissed the ground. It was very moving.

1990 trip to Israel

We had dinner in the huge dining room at our Jerusalem hotel on Friday, our first night there. After dinner, a band played lively Israeli music. Many of us started dancing in the aisles. My first thought was embarrassment—what will *They* think? Then it suddenly dawned on me! I didn't have to worry about what *They* would think. They were *Us*—the waiters, the musicians, the patrons—we were all Jewish! It dawned on me that I had unconsciously always censored myself in concern about what non-Jews would think about Jews. It was a great feeling to be in the majority for once! How it must be for Blacks in the United States to always be in the minority, having to live a dual consciousness.

This was soon after Russians had been allowed to emigrate, and the Jewish Ethiopians had just started arriving. Our itinerary included visiting a new Russian neighborhood, with dinner at a Russian home. During the dinner, I sat next to a recently arrived immigrant who spoke some English. I was appalled when he referred to the Arabs as animals, swine! How will there ever be peace when people have such prejudices?

I asked if we could also meet with some Ethiopians, so the tour leader arranged a visit to a training school for Ethiopian youth. I wondered whether any would go to college or if they were all being tracked into manual vocations. I was told that their lack of education made it unrealistic for them to pursue an academic track. Perhaps they were right, but I feared that was the beginning of a color-caste society.

Ruth Messinger and I, two single women, began sitting next to each other on our bus rides and realized we had both grown up in New York. We talked about our work, about advocacy, and social justice. A highlight of the trip was when she invited me to accompany her to a meeting with Israeli feminists in Jerusalem. One woman was an Orthodox member of the Jerusalem City Council and a feminist!

Some recounted their experiences at the Oslo Peace Conference, where they had met, behind the scenes, with the Palestinian Woman. Many of their ideas finally emerged in the final agreement, but of course they received no credit. They also recounted how the Palestinian women wanted to understand how the role of women in Israel had changed. There had been much talk about equality at the beginning of the State, but now the gender roles had hardened. They wanted to avoid the same process occurring in Palestine.

The Israelis said there were three reasons. One was the takeover by Likud, a very conservative party. The second was the influx of Sephardic Jews from the Arab countries after independence, who had never been exposed to Enlightenment values of equality. The third may have been the recent influx of Russians, who did not have a tradition of democracy and equality.

In addition to seeing the usual tourist attractions: swimming in the Dead Sea, climbing up to Masada, and spending a day at the chilling Holocaust Museum, we were driven to the edge of the West Bank. There, Ariel Sharon, who was not in government at that time, entered our bus, showing us how close we were to the Jordanian border and how their missiles could easily hit Tel Aviv or any other place in Israel. I was angry that the tour had set us up to be exposed to what I found to be a propaganda speech.

At the end of the tour, I took another three days on my own to visit Eilat, on the Red Sea, where I had a chance to do the most glorious snorkeling. My hotel was a block from the beach. Just walking a few feet into the water, you see a deep drop-off. I would spend an hour snorkeling along the side of the drop-off, seeing the most brilliantly colored fish, corals, and other sea creatures. When I was leaving Eilat, I was questioned at the airport.

"What were you doing here?" "Where were you staying?"

"Do you have your hotel receipt?"

After some trembling and fumbling, I found it, at which time they took my passport and receipt and withdrew to a room behind the counter. I was frightened and angry. I had to get to Jerusalem to connect with my plane back to New York. What a macho society! Harassing me simply because I'm a single woman traveling alone. After about ten long minutes, they returned and allowed me to board. I later learned I had been profiled. Apparently, some American young women were used by Arab men to carry material or information. At the time, I was just glad I was going home. This was another international trip that helped me learn so much about the world and also about myself.

After my two years at the Department, another election was held, and Bob Gaffney, a Republican, defeated Halpin. Immediately, I was pressured to resign, including a column to that effect in *Newsday*. During a candidate debate, Gaffney had expressed his dismay that a social worker headed the Department of Social Services! The commissioner position is a five-year position, specifically to remove it from political turnover.

I immediately requested a meeting with the new County Executive. I explained that I was not a therapist or direct practitioner; I had managed organizations and taught management and administration. I also told him about my goal to help women leave the welfare system through education and jobs that would enable them to support their families. At the end of the conversation, he said, "I think we can work together," and I agreed.

I thought everything was fine until about a week later when a Republican legislator introduced a proposal to remove several of my top staff who were all Democrats. I was incensed and returned to see Gaffney. He said the department was top-heavy, and they needed to economize. I replied that most positions receive a 75% match from federal and state sources. If he wanted to save money, he should not micromanage but give me a target number and let me decide which positions to cut. He replied that I should send him such a list. I returned to my office and prepared a list with some Republicans who had previously been put in administrative positions, who I thought were unproductive. The result was that I was allowed to keep three of the top people I did not want to lose; one who had been a Democratic political appointee was demoted, and I had to give up some vacant positions.

In 1991, I was approached by some colleagues organizing a trip to a social work conference in the Soviet Union. It seemed that with *perestroika,* the Communist Party youth workers, the *Komsomol,* were trying to reinvent themselves as social workers and "social pedagogues." The trip would be for educators and practitioners, with half the time at the conference in Artek, a youth camp on the Black Sea, followed by a few days in Moscow. There, we would meet with the psychology faculty, whose director was attempting to reorient their curriculum to social pedagogy. I was delighted to go.

We didn't get visas until the last minute as things were changing rapidly under Boris Yeltsin, who had just followed Gorbachev as president. Finally, we were on our way but had to change planes in Prague. When we arrived, the connecting flight to Moscow wasn't posted, so the group's two leaders went to look for our gate. After several minutes, they returned, telling us there were no flights to Moscow because there had just been a coup.

"Stop kidding around; we're tired and jetlagged!"

"No, no kidding, it happened, and we're stuck here in Prague."

A few days later, the coup was over, and we were off, changing planes in Moscow for Odessa, near the Artek camp. Once we arrived, we got the royal treatment. Every morning, we attended workshops or lectures with simultaneous English translations. Our colleagues attending the conference were *Komsomol* (youth) workers from Latvia, Lithuania, and the Ukraine. These workers had a social development rather than a therapy approach. For example, they taught their youth sign language so they could reach out and connect with the hearing-impaired.

Lunch was a daily banquet with wine, vodka, and toasts made by all. In the afternoon, we went on a tour or to the nearby pristine beach for a swim. Dinners were another banquet with more drinking. Our translator, a young Jewish Russian woman, remarked that her people didn't have enough food, but we were given all sorts of meats at every meal. She also told me that her son had wanted to go to McDonald's when it first opened in Moscow. The line was a block long, and a "happy meal" was equal to a week's salary.

It became apparent that no love was lost between our colleagues and the Soviets. A lot was going on sub-rosa that we didn't really understand. The highlight of the Artek visit was the program on the last day in the large stadium where the children and youth attending camp assembled. When the Soviet and American flags were raised they all sang "This Land Is Your Land." I couldn't believe it! It was so moving and made me think that maybe we could achieve world peace through our youth.

Then, on to Moscow, where we were housed in a Komsomol hotel with a concierge (or guard) at the elevator on every floor. Her job was to take your key and know when you were coming and going. When we met with the director and faculty in a classroom of the psychology department at Moscow University, I was reminded of faculty meetings back home. Obviously, the faculty couldn't care less about the director's agenda for connecting with social work educators. The director invited all of us to come back as visiting faculty. One woman in our group agreed to teach an advanced casework practice class, which was laughable, as they had not even had introductory social work courses.

The next day, we were off to what had been billed as a press conference. We went to what looked like state fairgrounds in the U.S. We sat on the stage of a large auditorium. The audience might have had some journalists present, but many seemed religious or new-age types. I noticed a short man off-stage, and when I inquired who he was, I was told he had purchased the facility from the state. Privatization, it seemed, was in high gear.

I started my talk in a way I thought was respectful of their country. I pointed out some of the flaws in our social welfare system and applauded their universal health care and education. This was met with derision. Everything Communist was now bad. They wanted to be capitalists like Americans. By the end of the trip, I felt so negative about their culture and politics that I had no desire to return. This was an early hint at how Russia evolved after the demise of the Soviet Union.

Now, back in Suffolk County, another issue percolated. The Handicapped Preschool Program was one of the programs in my department. Why was it in our department? No rational reason. When funding had first been made available from the state and feds to provide services for infants and preschoolers, it was handled in the previous county commissioner's office. When the woman overseeing the program moved to the Department of Social Services, the program went with her.

Children were evaluated for their need for speech, hearing, physical therapy, or other services, and transportation was provided. It seemed like a boondoggle, as the evaluators also provided the services. It was not surprising that the costs mounted steadily. Moreover, the cost of transportation, which was being provided by BOCES, part of the County school system, cost more than the actual services for the program!

Evelyn, the Deputy County Commissioner, was concerned about the cost and learned that in the neighboring county, a different contractor was providing bus transportation for their preschool handicapped program at a fraction of our costs. I was asked to meet with them and negotiate a possible change. At the following Human Services Committee of the Legislature, during the opening period before the agenda items, I was taken by surprise when the BOCES principal asked to speak. He complained that I had not met with him to discuss transportation costs.

Just "coincidentally," one of the members of the Legislature was a board member of BOCES. I had no forewarning of this but tried to calmly and rationally explain that I was trying to save the county money and would be happy to meet with the principal. I did, and suddenly their price for transportation services fell dramatically, in line with the other company. I decided it was wiser to stick with them. Another crisis averted!

Would you think that was the end of it? No way. About a year later, I was called before a grand jury examining the BOCES transportation contract. I was assured that I wasn't being investigated, but rather that the county legislator was, for conflict of interest. Nevertheless, I was cautioned that you never know what may happen once a grand jury meets. They will want to indict someone!

I was advised to get a lawyer, but when I asked the County to provide one, they said they could not do so since it was a criminal investigation. I ended up finding an excellent Republican attorney at my own expense. He advised me how to handle myself when I was questioned.

As you can imagine, it was an anxiety-producing experience in a large room with over thirty jurors in stadium-type seating and me on a raised platform in front of them. I could not have an attorney present but could ask for a recess to consult if I chose to. My attorney advised me not to, as it would look like I had something to hide. I had been prepared well, answered the questions clearly and truthfully, and had no negative consequences, aside from about $700 out of pocket for his fee. However, I realized it was probably time to leave, as they might find other ways to harass me.

My term was five years, and I was in my fourth year. When I took the position I had retained the deanship and my tenured full professor position at Stony Brook. After two years, I gladly relinquished the dean position, as it had been nothing but aggravation, but the Vice President had assured me I could come back. "Anytime you get tired of that circus, just give me a week's notice," I told Mr. Gaffney I would resign but asked for time to work out my arrangements. So, after four years, I returned to Stony Brook in 1993.

Suffolk County Dept of Social Services farewell party – 1993

CHAPTER 11

Another Health Crisis, Extraordinary Trips and End of an Era

Now, in my early fifties, I was ready for new challenges. After leaving the County position in 1993, I had applied unsuccessfully for several university dean and president positions. Not wanting to join a Republican governmental position at city, state, or federal levels, I reluctantly returned to my tenured full-professor ten-month position at Stony Brook. This coincided with the birth of my first grandchild, so having summers off to be with family in Seattle was a boon. Never before had I had summers off—neither as a dean nor at Boston University, where I had taught summer school to augment my salary.

Returning to Stony Brook was jumping back into the frying pan. When I gave up the deanship after two years at the County, the acting dean was given the position permanently. There had been no search; her PhD was from a then non-accredited online university, and I believe she felt threatened by my return. She was also upset because my salary was equal to or greater than hers, until she prevailed on the vice president to remedy her situation. She gave me an office far from the main area of faculty offices, out in a hallway near the bathrooms, where I shared the office suite with a grants program only tangentially related to the school. It seemed my aggravation at Stony Brook would never end.

She gave such a hard time to several of the tenured faculty who had given me such a hard time that they retired. She changed the system so that she had more power and used rewards and punishments to retain control in a way I never had. I had tried to use a feminist, inclusive approach to leadership. She told me she had learned from my "mistakes."

She assigned me to teach a year-long class at our NYC campus on Saturday mornings at 9:00 a.m. I told her I would take my turn as other faculty had and teach there, but only in the fall semester. As it turned out, I was able to stay at a friend's *pied a terre* each weekend and had a great time exploring the city. On Friday evenings, I would enjoy an ethnic dinner at little restaurants near the apartment. On Saturday, the class ended at 10:30 a.m. so I would spend the rest of the day attending book fairs or lectures and get half-price Broadway theatre tickets for the evening. I also enjoyed teaching these students, who worked in city agencies and had to take their course on weekends. As one faculty member used to say, "When you get lemons, make lemonade!"

One bright spot was that before retiring, Robert had proposed starting a Social Justice Center at the School and I was asked to lead it. This assignment was in addition to heading the social policy curriculum and teaching in our new doctoral program. Teaching had always been my first love and I was happy to have more time with students and to be freed from administrative responsibilities.

I was assigned a student assistant for the Center. My goal was to connect social work to social justice at the ground level. We developed a questionnaire for county legislative candidates and ran a social justice film festival. We also organized an annual conference, required for social policy students but open to other students and social work practitioners. We would identify state legislative issues with a social justice component (e.g., affordable housing, anti-gay discrimination) and invite speakers to present and provide talking points in a morning session.

In the afternoon, we separated into rooms on each of the four or five topics to role-play a legislative visit. A faculty member would role-play a legislator in each session. These gave students an experiential understanding of legislative advocacy, followed up in their policy classes with an assignment to visit a legislator. Advocacy for social justice is a key social work value, and I was thrilled to implement it and pass the torch to a new generation of social workers.

Ruth and MSW Stony Brook School of Social Welfare social justice march

I broke up the time at Stony Brook, first with a six-month visiting professorship and a few years later with a one-year sabbatical. Kay Dea, the dean of the University of Utah School of Social Work, invited me to be their Belle Spafford Visiting Professor for one year. Upon learning that my two issues of concern were poverty and family violence, he suggested I focus on family violence. My predecessor in the position, Naomi Gottlieb, had done a lot on poverty. "You know," he said, "we have a lot of family violence here in Utah, but people don't want to acknowledge it. It would be helpful to have an outsider raise the issue."

This program was funded by interest earned from an endowment, but because of the recession, they did not have enough to fund me for a full year. Instead, I was funded for one-week stays for three semesters followed by a six-month residency., I was flown in and housed for a week each time. This gave me the opportunity to meet key faculty and community members, develop an advisory council, and begin a research project.

The faculty and staff were welcoming and helpful, and I connected with the Jedi Woman, a community-based group of women in poverty. I learned that many members were survivors of domestic abuse and were on welfare. That gave me the impetus for a large research project studying the connections between the two. Over three years, I interviewed women in Utah, Washington State, and Long Island, culminating in conferences both in Salt Lake City and Long Island; I gave speeches at local and national conferences, and in 1999, published a book, *Battered Woman, Children and Welfare Reform: The Ties That Bind*.

Book cover Battered Woman, Children, and Welfare Reform

I found Utah to be a fascinating place, almost a theocracy. Most of the state and national elected officials are Mormons, most of the downtown area is owned by the Church of Latter-Day Saints, and once you leave Salt Lake City and Park City, which are somewhat cosmopolitan and diverse, you enter a closed society where outsiders are not tolerated. Although polygamy was officially banned for Utah to become a state, I was shown pockets, even in Salt Lake City, where group marriage existed. When I asked a progressive woman why this was tolerated, she replied that some women liked it. They could share the chores of childcare, cooking, working outside the home, and being a sexual partner—one didn't have to do it all. In contrast, one of the young Jedi women I interviewed, who had agreed for her husband to take a second wife, found the situation intolerable. Where the two had previously been partners, he became so domineering that she finally fled the marriage.

Health Issues

On my return to Stony Brook, my relationship with the dean improved, and I was finally moved to a large office with a window in the far corner of the second corridor of faculty offices. I went for my annual physical in 1999, and the doctor found something questionable in my blood. You have antibodies to Hepatitis C. I didn't even know that existed. How could I have gotten Hep C? I never used needles for tattoos or drugs. My doctor ordered a sonogram to see if my liver looked abnormal, and when they looked, they found a tumor in my right kidney. I was lucky! The liver is on the right side of the body. I would probably be dead by now if it had been my left kidney.

Of course, I didn't feel lucky. Here I had been, a perfectly healthy fifty-nine-year-old, and now I suddenly was diagnosed with two life-threatening illnesses. Having escaped AIDS, would I now die from one of these? I was planning to visit Seattle for the summer again, but the urologist I saw said, "I STRONGLY urge you to have the operation for the tumor immediately." He added that he would do a liver biopsy simultaneously to see how far the Hep C had advanced.

The next week, I was operated on at Stony Brook Hospital. Strangely, I don't remember being terribly frightened or depressed. I was just dealing with what I had to do. Garth and family, who had planned to join me in Seattle, came to Long Island instead. They visited me daily but also had time to visit beaches in the area and tried to have some vacation for Elise, who was only two years old. Because I had been a dean, many hospital administrators knew me. The heads of Nursing and Social Work visited me. I was treated exceptionally well. I would hope all patients get that kind of caring treatment, not just those with "pull." Still, I was grateful to have been in good hands. The surgeon visited me the day after the operation, July 4. He was in Bermuda shorts, probably on his way to a picnic.

The dean was most solicitous and offered to give me a leave of absence. I knew that just sitting around at home for five months would be very depressing, so after a few weeks of recuperation, I asked to return with a lighter schedule. I taught my classes sitting down and found myself tiring quickly, but I was happy to be able to function.

When I called for the pathology report, I got an unclear message. Finally, my doctor said it was not a renal carcinoma, which was what they had suspected of a tumor the size of a lemon. Instead, it was a rare renal oncocytoma. Doctors disagreed as to whether it was benign or a slow-growing cancer. In any case, both the kidney and adrenal glands had to be removed. Thankfully, it was still fully encapsulated, and I enjoyed a full recovery.

As for Hep C, the biopsy showed only minor scarring at the margins of the liver. The doctor recommended monitoring it. He thought that might have been caused by the initial infection and had not progressed. He did another test in 2002 and found more damage to the liver, so he recommended going on antiviral medications. In 1999, the medications had been only thirty percent effective, and tests were indeterminate as to which strain of Hep C I had. I asked him to rerun the test, and he found that I had the less common strain that required only six months instead of a year of treatment. It was another lucky break among all the bad luck I have had. I had to take both interferon and ribavirin, injecting myself daily with the first. I had been warned of possible side effects, and my sister visited for the first week, but the side effects were not so bad then. They were cumulative. At one point, I developed anemia and had to go on medication for that. I was fatigued and developed a terrible, itchy rash on my abdomen near the end of treatment.

However, the good news was that after only three months, there was no sign of the disease, and after six months, it appeared to be, if not cured, then in regression. (I am tested yearly and still have no signs of its return!) It was a frightening, horrid experience, but I have overwhelming gratitude to Dr. Elling, who with his wife, his nurse practitioner, was with me through it all. He once said, "Let us do the worrying for you." I don't know how I would have survived emotionally without that support.

My sister said, "Once more, you've dodged the bullet!" I am grateful for my life and have tried to make the most of it. I have become more loving and grateful to the people in my life, having survived the danger of AIDS, as well as potential death from Hepatitis and a kidney tumor.

A wise person once said we cannot control everything that befalls us, but we can choose how we handle them. I have had my share of tragedy, professional aggravation, and health crises, but I have not become bitter. I decided long ago at Stony Brook that I would not let the negativity change me. I am willing to accept suffering when I must, but I am resilient. I usually can finally find the positives and see myself as a strong woman, a survivor.

In 2000, I was due for another sabbatical. I wanted to go to Italy or another European nation, but my mother, who lived in Seattle, was now in the third stage of Alzheimer's, and we knew she would not last much longer. My sister Gale had been her primary caretaker and arranged for 24/7 in-home help. It wouldn't be fair to her for me to go off, and I also wanted to be there with my mother.

So, I took my sabbatical in Seattle, teaching an organizational change class and continuing my family violence research at the University of Washington, where years before I had gotten my MSW. I had friends at the university and made other friends, rented a tiny houseboat on Lake Union, from which I could swim and kayak, and between school and visits with Mom, had a great time. I taught a course to masters- levels students and conducted the research I had started in Utah, interviewing women who had been abused by their partners and had utilized public welfare.

Mom died on July 12, 2001, and my sabbatical ended that summer. My only regret was that I was not with her at that moment before she died. A few days earlier, she developed pneumonia, and Gale and I decided not to have her hospitalized. We knew it would not do any good, possibly only temporarily delaying the inevitable and would make her disoriented and frightened. She tended to paranoia, especially in unfamiliar surroundings.

We brought in hospice, and Gale and I took turns being with her. I had been there all afternoon, and the hospice nurse who visited expected Mom to have a few more days, so I went to an outdoor concert with a friend. At intermission, I called the house and was mortified to learn that Mom had died. That afternoon, I had told her it was okay for her to go, that Gale and I would care for each other as she had always admonished us to do. Maybe that was why she finally was able to let go. Still, I had wanted to hold her soft, frail hand, touch her bony shoulder, and kiss her soft cheek one last time before she took her last breath.

Cuba

One day, after returning to Stony Brook after my sabbatical concluded, I got a call from Sonia, a former student who had helped organize the National Association of Puerto Rican and Hispanic Social Workers. "Aren't you going with us to Cuba?" she asked. I didn't know anything about it, but I immediately signed up when she told me of this one-week trip her organization had planned to meet with family and children's mental health workers. We would be a group of twenty-two social work educators and practitioners, of whom eighteen were of Puerto Rican or other Hispanic heritage.

One of the first things I noticed was the Cuban people. They seemed at ease, not what one would expect if it were a totalitarian society. When I heard about the trip, I asked to meet with some government social policymakers. On Monday, we were ushered into a large conference room in a main government building where the head of Social Services and her key staff spent several hours with us, speaking openly about their system and its challenges and welcoming our questions. Because eighteen of our group spoke Spanish, we didn't have to rely solely on a translator, so we were confident in what we heard. We were impressed with the level of human services offered and the outreach to people's homes. On the one hand, it is intrusive to privacy, but on the other, it personalizes the interactions and helps identify problems and find solutions.

After the Cuban Revolution, social work was shunned as a Western, capitalist invention not needed in a Socialist country, but they recently reintroduced it. The first cohort in this new social work program had embarked on a research project to identify needs. Now, they were returning to the classroom to hone their skills. They were organized by both neighborhoods and ages of clients and were all generalists. They would meet in the homes of those they worked with (not called clients) who could knock on the social worker's door if they needed help.

We had an opportunity to meet with these "new" social workers and learned how they were being trained. All take courses in law, do home visits and link needs-based research with practice. I was impressed with what I consider a feminist approach to treating those you work with as partners, not objects.

We had the freedom to walk around or take the old 1952-model taxis wherever we wanted. To my amazement, people on the street were friendly, except one day when I tried taking a photo of a man lying drunk on the street. I was shocked when my elbow was suddenly shoved by someone who cried out, "No!"

Sonia and I decided to visit the University of Havana. I was impressed with the campus: late 19th-century brick buildings set on a spacious, grassy campus looked like it could be any large American university. We met a young graduate student couple and learned a lot from them. All colleges, law, and medical schools are free, and all required textbooks are loaned. However, students, however, are required to pay for food and lodging. Even if they live at home, they are not contributing income to the family, so financial constraints can still limit attendance. We found that Cubans practice their values not only by sharing textbooks but also with government vehicles. Anyone driving such a vehicle is required to stop and pick up any passengers going their way. The people own them, and they have a right to use them.

Next on our crowded itinerary was a two-day trip to Oriente Province, where we visited a residential facility for those with HIV or AIDS. We met with several residents, but I have no way of knowing if they were representative of the community or handpicked to give a positive picture. They said the government had contained the epidemic early by requiring isolation of all those infected. It isn't mandatory now, but we were told many prefer living here in this community because, as gay men, they have the freedom to pursue their lives. At home, in small, crowded apartments with families who were often judgmental, they did not have that freedom.

Back in Havana, we visited a children's psychiatric facility in an old mansion in a lovely part of town. These old mansions had been confiscated from their wealthy owners after the Cuban Revolution, and many now were public buildings. We met with the head of the facility, a psychiatrist who had started the program soon after the Revolution, with Castro's blessing.

Her model is collaborative, and she works closely with her staff of nurses, social workers, and psychologists. She seemed respectful and egalitarian in her approach, keeping with the Revolution's values of non-elitism. Preferably, children are treated in the least restrictive setting, in their communities, which all have neighborhood health services. This hospital is for those needing more intense services, and mothers can stay there with their children.

Until recently, because of the American boycott, they had no access to psychotropic drugs, so they used talk therapy, acupuncture, massage, and herbal medicines. Those are still preferable, but recently, Cuba has partnered with foreign companies to build pharmacological facilities, hiring Cuban workers, which will revert to Cuban ownership after twenty or thirty years.

While health and education services are free, available, and of high quality, the infrastructure is poor. Housing is dilapidated, and families must often share small quarters. It is the government that determines where you will be placed. Food is scarce, although monthly rations are provided for rice, beans, eggs, milk, and other necessities based on family size. Transportation is another problem, we were told, especially outside of Havana. We saw the ubiquitous old autos in the city. The "camel" buses are two cars long and fully packed with passengers, some even holding on to the outside.

In summary, I was impressed with the state's social, health, and educational services and their attempt to infuse their egalitarian values into these services.

Sarasota

Every winter, after my friend Bev and her husband Hal had retired from Stony Brook, she would invite me to their winter home in Sarasota. "Come down, you'll love it. There are classes, concerts, interesting things to do," she'd say. And every year, I would turn up my nose at the idea of Florida. To me, Florida was the Miami area where old Jewish relatives went to play pinochle and canasta and die. I wasn't interested.

Then, in May 2003, she told me someone she knew was buying her sister Bunny's three-bedroom place because Bunny had to go into assisted living, and the woman was selling her two-bedroom, fully furnished unit. I went down to see it and immediately fell in love with Pelican Cove, the condominium development where Bev lived.

Sunset at Pelican Cove, Sarasota

As soon as I entered the gate, driving through the canopy of melaleucas bordering the road and turning to see live oaks with Spanish moss dangling from their limbs, I was overwhelmed. I explored Sarasota and learned of their opera, concerts, dance, and theatre. Then I decided to explore Siesta Key—if I'm going to buy down here, maybe I should be right on the water. I have always loved the beach, ever since our family used to go to Coney Island. Siesta Key was too touristy, and Pelican Cove was beautiful, but I didn't like the woman's unit; it was too dark. I went home without making any decision.

In December, after classes were over, I returned to see if Pelican Cove was as magical as I had remembered. It was better! I looked at a few units and made an offer on a two-bedroom, second-story corner unit with high ceilings and a clerestory window. The purchase was consummated in March 2004.

My plan had been to eventually retire to Seattle, where my daughter and her family, and my sister lived. I lived there for six years in the Sixties, had done my sabbatical there, and spent most summers there since my granddaughter was born. I had been young, working, going to school, and raising a family when I lived there. I didn't have time for many outdoor activities.

In later years, when I visited in the summers, the weather was good, and I swam and kayaked. But when I did my sabbatical there, I was aware of how early the sun set, how dark it got, and how rainy and gloomy it was for a good part of the year. Is that where I want to spend my retirement? Or should I go to Sarasota, where I could swim, be outdoors, and enjoy the warm weather all year long? More and more, the winters were feeling too cold, and I found myself wearing socks to bed for six months of the year.

I turned sixty-four a month after I bought the condo and made a proposal to the vice president, strategically deciding to approach him before approaching the dean with my plan. I proposed going to 51% time to preserve my tenure and benefits, working full-time in the fall semester, and taking the spring semester off. I could go on to Social Security when I turned sixty-five. With that and my half-salary, I would have sufficient income. I don't buy many toys or clothes-I need just enough to travel, have dinner with friends, and go to concerts and plays when I want. He asked if I would be on-site or working from Florida during my semester of classes. Of course, I would live up here and come to Stony Brook to teach. Then he said,

"You know a doctor recently asked me for something like this, and I turned him down."

Oh no, I thought, that's that.

"But," he continued, "you are a person of integrity, so I will permit it. For how long?"

I thought it would be two to four years with the possibility of returning to full-time. When I approached the dean, she was delighted, seeing visions of my half-salary that could probably buy a full-time junior faculty member or several adjunct instructors.

In the winter of 2004-5, I began my life in Pelican Cove. That first year, the retirement plan wasn't in effect yet, so I stayed there just one month during winter break and rented it out for the rest of the season. Then, in December 2005, as soon as the semester ended, I came down on the Amtrak car train with papers to grade and my car full of whatever I would need. I've always loved train travel.

I purchased a reclining coach seat, and had no one sitting in the seat beside me. I had dinner in the dining room, the table set with a linen tablecloth and a complimentary glass of wine. The following morning, I watched the Southern landscape from my window before having a full breakfast, departing, retrieving my car, and driving over the Sunshine Expressway to Sarasota.

Once there, I swam, did some line-dancing, read, worked on my article on women for the *Social Work Encyclopedia,* and was flown back to Stony Brook in February for our annual Social Justice Conference, which I was responsible for planning. I continued this schedule not for two years nor four but for five years.

In 2008, I attended the International Association of Schools of Social Work Conference in Durban, South Africa, where I gave a paper on social work and social justice. The paper attempted to define social justice and described how I had been working at my center to operationalize social justice values into social work practice. The conference was stimulating; I renewed old acquaintances, made new friends, and had the opportunity to meet with Abye, dean of the new School of Social Work at Addis Ababa University in Ethiopia. The year before, I had been approached by a colleague at the University of Michigan about being part of a group of educators to help start up this new doctoral program. At that time, I declined, but now he invited me to teach there.

Presentation on Social Justice and Social Work, International Assn of Schools of Social Work, Durban, South Africa – 2008

"I just obtained a grant until next March to pay expenses for foreign faculty members to come there to teach."

He wisely invited American and European faculty to teach courses there instead of sending doctoral students abroad. What often happens is that once abroad and educated, graduates choose not to return, and their home countries lose the benefit of their training. His offer worked perfectly with my new schedule at Stony Brook. I arranged to come the following January, the best time of year in that climate. He wanted me to teach a doctoral class and said I could decide what to teach and how to schedule it. I decided to teach a course on Social Problems, Social Policy and Program Development, and would teach four full days a week for four weeks. That is the equivalent of an entire semester course at Stony Brook. I decided to stay a week after the course was completed to tour the country on my own.

Ethiopia

Before leaving home, I was filled with anxiety. Days before leaving, I still didn't know where they would put me up or who would meet me at the airport. Here I was, about to travel almost 10,000 miles over almost three days and countless time zones to a strange country, and all these arrangements seemed up in the air.

The Friday night before I left, my friend Kayla urged me to attend Shabbat services at her new congregation. I attended and was surprised when the student rabbi officiating invited me up to the *bimah* (the lectern). When I approached, she put her hands on my shoulders, recited something in Hebrew, and then translated it into English. It is a prayer for travelers. I never knew there was such a prayer. She gave me a copy, and I took it with me—it must have worked because I got there and returned safely!

After a long, grueling trip with several plane changes, I finally arrived in Addis Ababa and was greeted by Beyene, the School's driver. I was so relieved that I kissed him on both cheeks, which is the proper greeting in that country. He took me to the small hotel that would be my home for the next month.

I met Deborah for lunch the next day. An American, she had been working in Addis for several years. As I took a taxi to meet her, I was unnerved by the sights on the edge of the road. In the reddish dirt, among pieces of broken concrete and rock, men and women, homeless or beggars, were huddled. One woman especially haunted me. She could have been any age from thirty to sixty— it was impossible to tell because of her condition. Lying on top of a dirty blanket square in the dirt, she raised her head slightly to beg. A few coins were beside her body. She was literally skin and bones and was probably dying of AIDS.

The following day was Monday and my first day teaching. The School of Social Work was not housed on the main campus but about a twenty-minute drive in the suburbs. The Akaki campus was new, in what had been a sprawling office complex with several new two-story buildings. Everything else on campus was closed for the Timkat holiday, and few students were on campus. I decided it was pointless to start teaching that day, so I got a ride back to Addis to see the Timkat celebration. Timkat is an important festival. Ethiopians believe that the actual Ark of the Covenant (Ten Commandments) resides in the temple in Axum, an ancient city in the north of Ethiopia, and the ceremony of Timkat, held throughout the country, symbolizes it.

I returned to the city with Beyene. Suddenly, I saw a huge crowd, many poor men wrapped in blankets and women in white garments, covered from head to foot. He got the man controlling crowds to let us up to the front. People were shoving and touching but were good-natured. I kept saying, "*Yikita*," excuse me. Many were dancing, some with umbrellas.

Then, I climbed up some steps to observe the process from above. The women would ululate at intervals of the clapping and chanting, while men were dancing and chanting in a circle, with a drummer in the center. We saw groups in different colors, one of young girls in green and men in white with long colored sashes. This continued for quite a while as this mad procession was making its way toward the church. Then came the head priests in splendidly decorated gowns and capes, carrying gorgeous gold-threaded umbrellas high over their heads; in front of them, a young man hoisted a large red, green, and yellow Ethiopian flag. Finally, at the very end of the procession, three men on either side of it carried the "ark."

Timkat festival, Nairobi, Kenya – 2009

I am so grateful that I was able to experience this, as well as so many other unforgettable scenes, from the huge Addis marketplace, laden with fruits, spices, and clothing in a riot of colors, to the historic churches and monasteries, decorated with brightly colored illustrations of Biblical stories. I saw men bent over their walking sticks, others herding goats in the street or paddling in papyrus canoes, which made me feel as if I had stepped into Biblical history. The landscape also varied from acacia-dotted, scrub-like, brown flatlands with little villages to the impressive waterfall that marked the beginning of the Blue Nile. On a weekend trip while driving south, I saw dromedaries, hippos, huge marabou storks, and thousands of brilliantly colored flamingoes.

Soon after my arrival, Obama's inauguration was approaching, so I called the U.S. Embassy to see if there would be a party and if we could get invited. No party—the Bush administration was still in charge, and they weren't celebrating, so the next day, I hosted a little party in my hotel suite with three Scandinavian visiting faculty, Emebet, the associate dean, and myself. Everyone was impressed with Obama's speech. I have never felt so proud to be an American, sitting with people from other nations to watch the inauguration of a Black president, my president!

One Friday, I was invited to a Shabbat dinner in the home of Rick Hodes, an American doctor who has worked in Ethiopia for several years. He works at the Mother Theresa Clinic, diagnosing children with severe spinal disorders and, when necessary, arranging for their operations with international doctors. He has sheltered and fostered many of these children, some for a few weeks and some permanently.

I also had the unusual opportunity to witness the wedding of one of the graduate students in the largest Ethiopian Orthodox cathedral in Addis and visited the Fistula Hospital, where poor rural women are treated for tears in the peritoneum. Once again, I was learning about the culture, the problems, and the human services in a country, so unlike mine.

Of my twelve graduate students, three were women—unusual in a nation where the average girl receives only a primary school education. They were accustomed to the European model of lecture instruction, but I involved them in a seminar where each had to research and present a social problem and then develop policies for addressing it. They learned from each other—some men challenged one woman who researched violence against women.

February 10 was the last day of class, and it was absolutely wonderful! After six hours of final student presentations, we had twenty minutes for wrap-up and feedback. I was overwhelmed by how positive they were. They appreciated my knowledge and experience and that I had come to Ethiopia to teach them; I had sent readings and a syllabus ahead of time and shared my American examples with them (always prefacing it by saying it might not be appropriate for the Ethiopian context). They also appreciated my democratic style and my "sympathetic" way. They were also surprised that I had covered everything on the syllabus. One commented,

"You don't tell us we are wrong. You are gentle, but maybe in the US, that works; here, you need to be clearer when someone is wrong."

I replied that saying you are wrong can be counterproductive and rarely is something clearly right or wrong. Overall, it was very reaffirming for me and my teaching style.

Then, it was my turn, and I told them what a joy it had been to teach them. They're smart, hard-working, and committed, and I predicted they would be the social welfare leaders of their country. Already semi-retired, this was one of my life's most fulfilling teaching experiences! I left Ethiopia on February 17, 2009, with incandescent memories of this amazing trip, especially the smart, friendly, gentle people I met.

I have followed the politics there and am grieved by the recent chaos engulfing that nation.

Retirement, Finally

Turning seventy in 2010, I knew it was time to leave Stony Brook. The students were getting younger, the technology more intrusive, and I wanted to go while people still wanted me to stay. I had seen too many professors past seventy, or even eighty, when they no longer perform optimally, stay on because there are no age limits. Don't be the last to leave the party!

In August, I retired from Stony Brook, sold my house, found a three-bedroom unit in Pelican Cove with a view of the Intercoastal, and moved down permanently, to paint, dance, do photography, and try using my right brain instead of all the intellectual left-brain activities of my former life.

Now, as a full-time resident, I felt I was obligated to get involved with my community. If I'm living in Florida, I should try to make it a better state. It was summer, and there were few activities in Pelican Cove, so I found a local NASW meeting. When I inquired about their legislative committee, I was told, "We don't have one. Would you like to chair the committee?" That started my involvement with the local and state professional organizations.

I also signed up for the county's Civics 101 class to learn about county government. That led to my appointment to the County Human Services Advisory Council, where, for six years, I visited and rated human service organizations seeking government contracts. I realized I must enjoy this kind of work, as I keep doing it, even when I'm not paid. The difference is that I do it on my own time and try to balance it with kayaking, swimming, seeing friends, attending cultural events, and traveling.

I chose Pelican Cove because I assumed I would remain single and was aware of the dangers of isolation after retirement. Pelican Cove had many single women and couples who were academics and politically progressive. I thought, "This is a place where I can always find companionship and a support system."

That first Christmas of 2010, I went to the holiday party myself. I already knew some people. Everyone was friendly, and I could dance with some of my friends' partners or husbands. The second year, I didn't want to go alone. Wolf, a social worker I had met at Pelican Cove, was good at getting people together. He invited me to his Sunday dinner group. First, we would assemble at his condo for drinks before going out for dinner. Among the guests was a tall, distinguished-looking older man with a striking blond woman. Later, I asked Wolf why the woman was with that old guy.

"Jim is a great guy, very smart and funny, and no, they aren't a couple, just friends."

So, when I decided that I wanted to find someone to accompany me to the holiday party, I called Jim. What did I have to lose? It didn't matter to me if he declined, but he didn't.

That was the start of a six-year relationship. He shared my love for classical music and opera. During the season, we would go out for dinner and then to the opera, concerts, or plays. Once a week, he would stay over on Saturday nights, and we'd have breakfast at my place, reading the Sunday *New York Times*.

Jim loved to travel, and every year, we went somewhere abroad. He planned and insisted on paying for these trips. His wife of over fifty years had died after several years of dementia, and he badly wanted a traveling companion. First, he chartered a sailboat in Tortola, and he and I sailed the British Virgin Islands. That fall, we journeyed to the Amalfi Coast, followed by a trip to France the next year. Subsequently, we embarked on a cruise through the Baltics, culminating in a two-week stay at a colleague's summer home in Crete. The last year he was unable to travel abroad, so we flew to Rhode Island to visit his family, drove to Cape Cod for a week, and then visited Boston for a few days with my friends.

Jim was eighty-two when I met him and had had three hip surgeries. His hip continued to give him trouble, and after our car accident in 2013, he fractured some spinal discs and discovered he had osteoporosis and arthritis. He found it increasingly painful to walk. That last trip to Cape Cod was a disaster. He couldn't do much and just wanted to stay in bed and rest in the little stuffy room in the B & B, without even a TV. I was responsible for lugging his scooter in and out of vehicles and on planes. During that trip, I had my first attack of irritable bowel syndrome, which, I later learned, can be triggered by stress.

The following winter, I went to a four-day writers' workshop in Key West. When I returned, I found him lying in bed in the dark. He was eating poorly and eventually was down to 141 pounds on his

6' frame. I involved his daughters, who arranged Meals on Wheels, which he sometimes neglected to eat. Finally, I pushed for some in-home help. They arranged this over his reluctance, and after two weeks, he fired the helper. He would get out of bed only when I came to take him somewhere. His daughters appreciated our relationship and said it was the only thing that kept him going.

Finally, we had a crisis. He had also declined my suggestion to get a panic button. He fell and couldn't get up for hours. He was disoriented and thought it had been days. I found him the next morning. His skin was fragile; so much blood was on the pillow and sheet where he had finally dragged himself back into bed. At that point, he agreed he could no longer care for himself. I immediately had him call his daughter, who had already been researching assisted living facilities in Rhode Island near her, and within a week, he left.

I visited him a few months after he settled in. He had already gained over ten pounds. The staff ensured he came down for meals and took his pills on time. It was a warm, friendly place with lots of activities and facilities. I took him to the building's movie theatre, the pub, the fitness facility, and even an art class. The calendar listed activities every day, but he seemed reluctant to partake in any. After the visit, I would call him because he no longer used his email. Sometimes, I would have to call two or three times before he found the phone and answered.

I visited him again the following summer, and while he seemed physically sound, he was not participating in anything. Even at meals, he did not enter into conversation, perhaps because without using his hearing aids, he couldn't follow the conversation. Aside from getting him out one evening to a nearby Italian restaurant (he loved pasta,) I couldn't persuade him to do anything, not even a piano concert at the facility. All he wanted to do was lie in bed, watch TV, and have sex.

When I returned from this unpleasant visit, I tried calling him, to no avail. So, instead, I wrote to him a few times but got no response. Although he was still physically alive, it was as though the Jim I knew was dead. I finally decided I had to break my emotional tie with him but kept in touch with his daughters. A few months ago, one daughter told me he had died at the age of ninety-one.

Iran

One day in early 2016, while scrolling through my e-mails, I came across one from *The Nation,* a progressive magazine. They were offering a new trip in their travel program to Iran. Iran? I couldn't believe Americans could visit, much less under the auspices of a lefty organization like *the Nation.* Intrigued, I checked the itinerary and learned it would be a cultural and historical trip to some major cities and ancient sites. It would not be political. The trip would occur in May, which would be a good time for me. Who would want to go with me? I checked with some friends, and Joan, my good friend from NY, with whom I had traveled to Peru in 2001, was as eager as I was.

My family and friends were shocked at my decision to go to Iran.

The comments ranged from "Aren't you afraid?" "You're so brave."

"Be sure to always stay with the group."

"I'll post your bail when you're arrested."

Like many Americans, they believed the media messages about repression in Iran and, knowing my adventurous spirit, were genuinely concerned for my safety. I appreciated this concern, but it didn't deter me from wanting to go and see things for myself. I've always been intrigued with this part of the world, partly because, as a Jew, I believe that is where my origins were.

This was an amazing trip. We were among the only 1,000 or so Americans who visited Iran that year. We started in Tehran and visited several museums. We then proceeded to Shiraz, a beautiful city close to Persepolis, the 2,500-year-old city of Kings Cyrus and Darius. From there, we bussed to Yazd, a desert city to which the Zoroastrians fled after the 7th-century invasion of Persia by Arabs.

The last city we visited before returning to Istanbul and home was Esfahan. This seemed a most livable city with a large square and reflecting pool in its center, flanked by mosques, a museum, shops, and a river with walking bridges. We were impressed by the ordinariness of daily life—children playing at the water's edge, families picnicking, strolling, napping, everyone friendly and welcoming us as Americans. I was impressed that the statues in the park were of poets and scholars, not generals or kings. When I learned there was still a Jewish population of 20,000 to 30,000, I visited their synagogue, arranged in Orthodox style with the bimah in the center and the women's balcony above.

The contrasts were unbelievable—Women in full black *chadors,* but stores showing mannequins in tights and apothecaries featuring makeup and condoms. Modern women drive, wear their hijabs back on their heads, showing dyed hair, and even get nose jobs and Botox injections to fill their lips.

We heard from Dr. H, an Iranian political scientist, on the last evening. Finally, we had a chance to talk about politics and ask questions. He said Iranians do not want another revolution like the one in 1979. They have seen the price paid, he said, and fear the chaos that could ensue. Instead, they are working for incremental change. He said the nation is vibrant and evolving but will remain an Islamic Republic. This was during the Obama administration when relations were warming. After that, the Trump administration withdrew from the nuclear agreement, which succeeded in strengthening the position of the right-wing in Iran. Now, the Biden administration is trying to restart the deal but has resistance from Congress.

I was now settling into my life in Sarasota. I was engaged in political activities, had a circle of women friends, was surrounded by the beauty around me, and was content, but then the 2016 election left me upset and dismayed. I found that the answer to despair is action, so I flew to Washington DC in January to join the millions rallying at the Capitol the day after the Trump inauguration. Despite the huge crowd of men and women, Black, white, Latinx, and Asians, it was very peaceful—and even jubilant. The feeling was that we wouldn't be stopped and we won't give up! When I returned to Sarasota, I joined almost weekly demonstrations for gun control, women's rights, and other social issues.

Rally after Trump Inauguration, Washington, DC, 2017

Downtown Sarasota Demonstration against Trump administration

In 2019, I was notified that I had been chosen to receive the Lifetime Achievement Award by the National Association of Social Workers. It was a great honor to have been selected from all social workers in the nation, and more so, as most social workers are clinicians, and my entire career has been working for organizational and social change. It was a glorious day when I received the award in Washington, DC, accompanied by my son, granddaughter and my friend Joan, who had been one of the nominators.

Lifetime Achievement Award presented by Gary Bailey, President of National Assn of Social Workers – 2018

My relationship with Jim had been the most positive, healthy, loving, conflict-free relationship I had ever had. I had felt some guilt about not continuing to be his caretaker, which I had essentially been for over a year, to the detriment of my health. I concluded that my responsibility to him was limited because this had not been a long-term marriage. When he went into the facility in Rhode Island near his daughters, I was seventy-seven and believed that would be my last relationship with a man. I was content. I had a loving family, good friends, a strong support network in Pelican Cove, and volunteer activities to which I gave my time, intellect, and energy. That was enough. But—you never know what life brings next.

CHAPTER 12

Epilogue

After that last visit with Jim and my futile attempts to communicate with him, I resigned myself to the end of that relationship and, I thought, to any other intimate relationships with men. I felt content. I had a full, satisfying life. I had good friends, volunteer work that gave me meaning, time to swim, kayak, and travel. Having been poor and living frugally, I've never been interested in having money, but I'm fortunate to have enough to last me, I hope, for the rest of my life. I will be content as long as I have enough to travel, buy subscriptions to cultural activities, and have dinner out occasionally. I've never been into buying flashy electronic toys or expensive jewelry, and I enjoy buying most of my clothes at consignment shops. I don't constantly spend money redecorating my home.

Both my children are in long, stable marriages. Lorena, now sixty-two, has been married to David for over thirty years and has two children: Sara, twenty-eight, and Alex, twenty-four. Things are going well for them, and we have a good relationship. Similarly, Garth has been married to Carolyn for over twenty-five years, and their two daughters, Elise and Emma, are twenty-six and twenty-two, respectively.

My relationship with them is rewarding. I am so grateful and happy to have my family. We exchange small gifts, and I always get beautiful and meaningful cards from them on my birthday and Mother's Day. This flies in the face of those who claim that divorced mothers cannot raise children who will be successful in marriage. If anything, I think my life became an incentive for both to maintain strong, loving marriages. The three older grandchildren have finished college, and my youngest granddaughter is entering her sophomore year. As my children have dealt with their children's growing up, I think they have become more appreciative of my challenges in raising them.

Who knows what the next decade will bring? I hope I am around and healthy enough to see how the lives of all four unfold. Whether I dance at their weddings, hold their babies, or watch them live different, alternative lifestyles, my love for them only continues and grows.

I thought this would end my story; however, it is not over! As I keep discovering, life brings us to yet another chapter—or more. When I became a full-time resident, I found and moved into my three-bedroom condo with a water view. Having lived on the water in Centerport, having a water view when I moved here permanently was important to me. I kept the first condo I purchased when I had discovered Pelican Cove as a rental unit.

In 2018, I once again had my two-bedroom unit available for rent, and a couple called to see it for a friend who wanted to rent in PC for the winter of 2019. They described a warm, intelligent, eighty-one-year-old who had lost his wife of fifty-eight years to cancer the previous year. On her deathbed, they told me, "She implored him to take the insurance money and go on a round-the-world trip." He was now in Japan. I started having fantasies of perhaps developing a relationship with him. The man's name was Joe.

They loved the unit and were sure Joe would want to rent it, but my condo office would not accept a faxed lease. He and I began to e-mail, and finally, he suggested that he would send me a down payment now to secure the unit and would sign the lease upon his return to the US in a few months. As we continued communicating, he told me he had a daughter living in Seattle. I have a daughter living in Seattle. His daughter is a potter. My sister is a potter. He grew up in New York, as did I, and he is also Jewish. He said he had no checks with him because he had his bank pay checks directly, but the check he promised had not come. "I'll take you to dinner when all this is over."

The check still didn't come. Now I was getting a bit leery. What was going on? Why did an eighty-one-year-old man want a second-floor unit that had not yet been redecorated and had no step-in shower? What about all these coincidences? Had he been stalking me online and found out about my life? What was the game? I couldn't figure out what was going on. Finally, Garth advised me to give him a cutoff date and, if I didn't get the check by then, to cancel the agreement. When I told Joe about this, he said, "Well, just give me your bank account and routing number, and I'll wire it directly to your bank." That was it! I freaked out. He was a scammer! I'd heard horror stories of men approaching older women and draining their bank accounts. I told him the deal was off! I was no sucker. He wrote asking me to return his check when it arrived. He mentioned that he planned to come to PC regardless but suggested we go to dinner and split the bill.

Yeah, I figured this was just a cool scammer saving face. All my friends had the same reaction I had when I told them the story. I rented the unit to someone else. About two days later, I received an envelope from the bank, which I steamed open to check the contents. It was the check, and I promptly returned it. That was the end of that … or so I thought.

Fast forward to December 2018. Our PC Year-Rounders' Club had its first potluck holiday brunch. About 100 people were there, some newly returned from up north. We all had name tags on because it's hard to remember names at our age. Afterward, I stood in the lobby, chatting with a few people I knew. An attractive blonde woman was seated, and a good-looking bearded man stood across from her and on my left. I assumed they were a couple.

Suddenly, the man pointed to his cheek and said, "Kiss me, Ruth." I assumed he must be someone I knew but had not remembered from last season, or maybe his beard was new, so I didn't recognize him. We're all pretty friendly in PC, so I gave him a peck on the cheek. Then he turned to me and said, "I'm Joe." I was so stunned I thought I'd fall through the floor, though I'm laughing aloud as I recount it now.

We arranged to go for coffee the next morning, but he called to cancel. Oh no, I thought, but then he quickly added that he was having a medical problem. I showed concern and offered to shop for him or take him to the doctor. That's what we do for each other in PC. I guess my caring moved him, so when his medical issue quickly turned out to be a false alarm, he suggested dinner on him. We went for dinner at Marina Jacks on Dec 28, and that was the beginning of my love affair with Joe.

We talked and talked. He would still get teary when talking about his late wife or when something would trigger a memory. We strolled on the harbor a few days later and talked more about our children, politics, and relationships. He wanted to start one, but I felt it was too soon. He was rushing things. He replied, "I'm almost eighty-two; I don't have any time to waste."

This was my first introduction to his wry sense of humor. As a former English major who ran an advertising agency, he does have a way with words. He had never before been in therapy and was in a grief counseling group at the local hospice. Now, he said I could be his "grief counselor." In fact, he rarely cries anymore and is moving on with his life. And by the way, there was no insurance money, and his wife never told him to travel around the world as she lay dying or at any other time. Although he was on a long international trip to see old friends, his friends made that up.

It's now been five years. We took a six-day road trip to New Orleans to test whether we could survive being together 24/7. We had a terrific time. He decided that rather than continue renting, he would buy a unit at PC so he could come and go from his home on Long Island whenever he wanted. Then, he decided to move here full-time. I visited him in his home in Mattituck, on the North Fork, that June of 2019 for two weeks, one of which I spent in his spare bedroom, working on this memoir and enjoying his cooking. I met his friends and drove west to Huntington to reunite with my NOW friends.

In August, when he was ready to move, I flew up for his going-away party, and then we spent an enjoyable road trip south, stopping in Cape May to see an old friend of mine, then along the Eastern shore visiting little coves where he and his family used to sail to, introducing me to she-crab soup (yummy!), until finally arriving back in Pelican Cove.

We are not the same, and are both clear that we could not live together. Our styles are too different. He likes order, and I'm an academic, and I live with clutter—piles of books, newspapers, and magazines. He works with his hands, and I with my head. And I've spent too many years in my own space. He's living alone for the first time and loving it. We talk every day and see each other several times a week. For our first anniversary, we went to dinner, and he surprised me by inviting the two couples who had first told him he had to meet me.

I still have my activities and friends, and he's made friends, repaired an old sailboat and makes whimsical clocks that he gives away. I've always maintained that I would not give up my female friends for a relationship with a man, but I have adjusted my schedule to make time for him. We have "PDs" (playdates) and "SOs" (sleepovers). And yes, he still makes me laugh.

We have lived through the COVID-19 virus. It limited our going out to events, so we watched the Metropolitan Opera, Netflix movies, and One-Day University online. Although I promised myself to cut back on political activities when I turned eighty, I still am active on Zoom. Having given up chairing the Sarasota Community Alliance Legislative Committee, I took on chairing the local League of Women Voters Health Committee. I was working (as it turned out, unsuccessfully) on getting Florida to finally accept Medicaid Expansion (one of only ten states that have not yet opted in.)

We met when I was seventy-eight. Maybe I'm a slow learner. I think I finally have relationships figured out. I learned that the important thing is for the other person to be a *mensch.* That means someone with integrity and a good heart, someone who cares for me and will care for me, someone I can Trust! Trust is a big thing for me. It has been a struggle for me to trust a man. Jim was a *mensch*, and thought it might be an insult when I called him that. He was an Irish Catholic from New England and didn't know what the word meant.

Joe is also a mensch. We have different styles but complement each other. We are similar in politics, in our acceptance of people who are different, in our love for classical music, opera, and dance, in having dinner with friends, and, at our age, in expressing our fun-loving selves. He's one of the few heterosexual men I know who likes opera, ballet, and modern dance. More than that, he is very loving and caring. He does have a heart condition but promised me five years and a quick death. I don't want him to talk that way, but I know nothing is forever, and at our age, who knows how long? Or even who will go first? But it's good now.

Ruth & Joe

As I write and rewrite this memoir, I realize I have lived an exceptional life and have faced several major crises. At a very young age, I made a bad choice, as so many women do. Finally, after great pain, I extricated myself from an abusive relationship. I thank whatever gods there be for my children. Yes, maybe I had them when I was too young to know any better, but having responsibility for them helped me make better decisions about how to live my life to care for and protect them.

Although I grew up poor, I had a stable family with middle-class values. My parents believed in education, work, honesty, and fighting for the underdog. While we didn't have many luxuries, we always had enough to eat and a roof over our heads. I was fortunate to live in an era when the government provided help—I never had to pay for my college or post-college education, and I was able to buy my first house with a minimum down payment.

I know I was also lucky by being entitled as a white woman. At twenty-six years old, with just a college degree, I was chosen to lead a local Seattle agency. Would I have been chosen had I been a Black woman? In fact, I learned after taking the job that a Black man with an MSW and more experience than I had was turned down for the same position.

I survived the fears I had when I finally applied for a divorce—terrified that Mel might reappear, that I might lose my children, but knowing I had to go through it. Similarly, when I had my illegal abortion, I was fearful. They say courage isn't not being afraid; it's doing what you need to do, even when you are afraid.

Bob's death from AIDS was a major crisis. I thought he was the love of my life, and it devastated my hopes for our future together, reawakened my distrust of men—and also put me in fear of losing my own life. I guess I have what the psychologists call "resilience." Both in leaving New York for Seattle as a young, poor woman with two babies and then with Bob's death, I was able to focus on just keeping on. I used what skills I had and did not succumb to self-pity, alcohol, or drugs to sedate myself. My work and my children both allowed me to focus on what I needed to do.

My next health crisis was my health. Suddenly, I had not one but two possibly fatal diseases. I had both a tumor in my kidney and Hepatitis C. It was a scary time, and the side effects of the hepatitis medications were no picnic! Still, I survived and am healthy, with no recurrence of either disease. Again, I weathered both through a combination of fortunate circumstances and my own resilience.

As the former dean, whose school was in the Health Sciences Center, I had access to the best health care, including the very generous health plan of the State of New York. I'm acutely aware of how many people, especially women of color, do not have access to quality health care. I see the issue of social and economic injustice in my own life. I wish everyone had the benefits I was fortunate to have.

Somehow, it seems I have a positive disposition. I am acutely aware of our nation's trouble and fear for my grandchildren's future. That is why I cannot and don't want to stop being involved in social action. I still get angry at injustice that I see around me. I may have slowed down somewhat (or maybe not), but I firmly believe that it is up to me—to us—to be part of the solution.

I remember studying with our rabbi for my bat mitzvah when he told us a story that when the world was created, it was evenly balanced between good and evil. It is up to each of us to make sure the balance is tilted toward the good. Also, as a Jewish child growing up immediately after World War Two, I cannot but think what I would have done if I were in Germany during the Nazi period. It is not a perfect analogy by any means, but the point is that I've always taken a personal responsibility to do my part to make the world a little better.

When I was young, I wanted to change the world; now, I just want to make the little part of my world—my community, city, and state, a little better for people. My father's ideology also reminds me that it is essential to make it better for us, the people, not for corporations.

In college, I studied the existentialists but did not really understand Sartre, who said, "Being is Becoming." I don't know what the next few years will bring, but I'm content and feel complete for now with becoming me—and I know my story is not over until it's over. Now I think I do understand that being alive is the act of becoming.

Acknowledgements

It is hard to believe this memoir is finally seeing the light of day. Writing it was easy—the memories and words poured out. It was converting it into a publishable book that was the real struggle

Starting this memoir five years ago, at age 78, I was satisfied with my life. Having retired from academic life, I was busy advocating for social justice and human services for women, children, and the poor. I had friends, my family was well, and I had just been honored with the National Lifetime Achievement Award from my professional organization. I had traveled throughout the world, had overcome personal health crises, death of loved ones and a harrowing early marriage and escape from my abuser. I decided it was time to set down my life experiences. I knew I wanted to document a record for my family. I was not sure who else my audience might be, but I was not interested in that question. I just knew I wanted to write.

So, that summer I rented a small condo on the beach in Siesta Key and completed five chapters. Then life intervened and it wasn't until the next summer that I completed five more chapters, and again put it away.. The third summer I completed it and started editing. Then, on a trip up north, I visited with my friend Paula, who read it and enthusiastically encouraged me to publish it. Young women need to read this and see how hard it was for you. You are a role model.She also said women our age would relate to my struggles as we began the fight for women's equality in the 60s and 70s. She made several important editorial suggestions, which I followed, but again put the manuscript away.

Now, at 83, and still in good health, I decided I needed to see it published before I die. I owe a debt of gratitude to the many friends who read and made comments, but I take all responsibility for any flaws in the final product. First, I must thank Paula Rayman for her extensive editing and even more importantly, giving me the confidence that this was worth publishing. Other friends read the final manuscript and made some important suggestions. I want to thank my good friend Joan Ohlson for her edits and title suggestions, my former doctoral student Cathy Carballeira for her enthusiastic response to the book and my fellow academic and travel buddy Carol Deanow for her edits, including an important fact correction. I also owe a tremendous debt of gratitude to Marcia Friedman, my almost-step-daughter, for creating the striking cover for the book. Thanks also to Ivis Anderson, April Matthews and their staff at ADP for final editing, formatting and putting it all together.

My heartfelt gratitude goes to Joe Friedman, my partner of five years, for calming me when my anxieties about the book were over-the-top and for always being there for me, in so many ways.

About the Author

Ruth Brandwein is Professor and Dean Emeritus at Stony Brook University. She has taught social policy at four universities, including holding an Endowed Chair at the University of Utah. She is the author of Battered Women, Children and Welfare Reform: The Ties That Bind, has published over 50 scholarly publications and has presented at national and international conferences. She also has served in leadership positions at the Council of social Work. Education and the National Association of Social Work, which granted her their Lifetime Achievement Award in 2018.

Ruth has been a tireless advocate for legislation concerning women, children and social justice at the local, state and national levels.

She has a PhD. in social welfare from Brandeis University, a Masters of Social Work from the University of Washington and and a bachelors degree in philosophy, magna cum laude, phi beta kappa, from Brooklyn College. Ruth is the proud mother of two and has four adult grandchildren

www.ingramcontent.com/pod-product-compliance
Lightning Source LLC
Chambersburg PA
CBHW051145120626
46547CB00012B/947